Civil Procedure in United States of America

Civil Procedure in United States of America

Scott Dodson

This book was originally published as a monograph in the International Encyclopaedia of Laws/Civil Procedure.

Founding Editor: Roger Blanpain
General Editor: Frank Hendrickx
Volume Editor: Wannes Vandenbussche

Wolters Kluwer

Published by:
Kluwer Law International B.V.
PO Box 316
2400 AH Alphen aan den Rijn
The Netherlands
E-mail: lrs-sales@wolterskluwer.com
Website: www.wolterskluwer.com/en/solutions/kluwerlawinternational

Sold and distributed by:
Wolters Kluwer Legal & Regulatory U.S.
920 Links Avenue
Landisville, PA 17538
United States of America
E-mail: customer.service@wolterskluwer.com

ISBN 978-94-035-4619-3

e-Book: ISBN 978-94-035-4629-2
web-PDF: ISBN 978-94-035-4639-1

This title is available on www.kluwerlawonline.com

The Author

An expert in civil procedure and federal courts, Professor Scott Dodson has published nine book titles, including with Oxford University Press and Cambridge University Press, and more than 140 shorter works appearing in *Stanford Law Review*, *New York University Law Review*, *Michigan Law Review*, *University of Pennsylvania Law Review*, *California Law Review*, *Virginia Law Review*, *American Journal of Comparative Law*, *American Journal of International Law*, *Law & Society Review*, and others. He has won numerous awards for his scholarship, his teaching, and his service. His scholarly writings have been cited in more than fifty court opinions, including by the U.S. Supreme Court, six state supreme courts, and ten different U.S. Courts of Appeals. His works have been downloaded nearly 100,000 times, and he was listed in the top-10 most-cited civil procedure scholars for 2010–2014 and 2016–2020. He has delivered lectures in Brazil, Croatia, Israel, Italy, Japan, Luxembourg, Portugal, the Netherlands, and Sweden. From 2021–2023, Professor Dodson hosted and produced the semimonthly podcast *Litigation Briefs: Media Shorts on Law and Courts*. In 2024, he was counsel of record for the petitioner in *Harrow v. Department of Defense*, winning a 9-0 reversal from the U.S. Supreme Court.

The Author

Table of Contents

List of Abbreviations

FAA	Federal Arbitration Act
FRCP	Federal Rules of Civil Procedure
FRE	Federal Rules of Evidence
IRS	Internal Revenue Service
MDL	Multidistrict Litigation
TRO	Temporary Restraining Order

List of Abbreviations

Preface

This wholly revamped and revised edition comes on the heels of recent but dramatic transformations in U.S. procedure. The last two decades have seen sea changes in jurisdiction, pleading, discovery, case management, aggregation, and jury trials. At the same time, U.S. procedure has started to detach itself from its parochial moorings and become more global. Perhaps readers will find this volume's description of U.S. procedure less exceptionalist than expected.

Prior editions of this volume were last completed in 2008 by Professor John Oakley and Professor Vikram Amar, two luminaries in the field of civil procedure to whom I am indebted. I have relied on their work as a solid foundation for this edition. Revisions reflect the evolving nature of U.S. litigation, not errors on their part.

General Introduction

§1. General Background

I. Americanism

1. The United States originated in a rejection of governmental power and sovereignty. The new nation intentionally departed from the customary monarchical tradition to institute a new form of government—a democratic republic founded on the idea that the people, not the rulers, are sovereign. A primary innovation was the adoption of the Constitution[1]—a written charter setting out limitations of government. The people of this new nation exhibited characteristics born of colonialism in a vast, isolated land—individualism, egalitarianism, and distrust of government—that inflected both the Constitution and the role of civil litigation in the new society.

II. Separation of Powers

2. The U.S. Constitution divides governmental power into three branches. It gives Congress the legislative power, and it divides Congress into two houses. The House of Representatives contains representatives apportioned by state population, while the Senate contains two senators from each state, regardless of population. Representatives are elected for two-year terms and senators are elected for six. The Constitution gives the President the executive power, elected to a four-year term. Congress can create agencies and bureaucracies to serve the President to assist with implementing the executive power. Finally, the Constitution gives the courts the judicial power.

3. In addition to dividing power among the federal branches of government, the Constitution also supplies additional checks. Of particular importance to this volume are the checks involving the judiciary. The judicial branch checks the other two branches by wielding the power to interpret the law and the legality of conduct, including the conduct of executive officials. In the famous case *Marbury v. Madison*,[2] the Supreme Court interpreted the Constitution to grant to the judiciary the

1. Convention capitalizes "Constitution" when referring to the U.S. Constitution but not to the state constitutions.
2. 5 U.S. (1 Cranch) 137 (1803).

power of judicial review—to pronounce a law to be unconstitutional. And in *Cooper v. Aaron*,[3] the Court held these powers to be binding on all other governmental officials.

4. To ensure that judges exercise these solemn powers faithfully and without undue influence from the political departments, the Constitution gives judges appointment for life, during good behavior, and protects their salaries from diminishment. The Constitution also guarantees the existence of the Supreme Court and establishes its original jurisdiction over certain classes of cases.

5. These constitutional powers and protections sit uncomfortably within a democracy that aims to hold government accountable to the people. Accordingly, the Constitution grants the federal courts only limited jurisdiction over specified classes of cases. In addition, the Constitution preserves the right to trial by jury in cases to which the jury right historically attached, thereby giving the people some say in the adjudication of disputed facts. Finally, the Constitution gives the other branches some checks on the judiciary. For example, judges are appointed by the President and confirmed by the Senate; they can be removed through impeachment by the House and conviction by the Senate. The courts must rely upon the executive branch to enforce their judgments. The courts have no power over their own finances; they must rely on funding from Congress. And Congress exercises plenary control over the business of the courts. Congress has the power to establish or abolish all lower federal courts, to set their procedures, and to control their jurisdiction. Congress even has the power to regulate the appellate jurisdiction of the Supreme Court. For these reasons, Alexander Hamilton called the judicial branch "the least dangerous branch" and "the weakest of the three departments."[4] He was not wrong; the history of the Supreme Court is the story of its delicate management of political capital.

III. Federalism

6. The Constitution establishes a unique federal structure. The national government operates alongside the separate, quasi-sovereign state governments. Every state has its own constitution establishing an elected legislature, an executive branch headed by an elected governor, and a judicial branch organized into tiers of trial and appellate courts. States enact their own laws—criminal laws, tax laws, healthcare laws, environmental laws, property regulation, tort laws, contract laws, employment laws, and more—that regulate their citizens' everyday lives in substantial ways. Those laws are enforced by the governor, and disputes arising under those laws may be heard by the state's courts.

7. States generally may structure their judiciaries as they see fit. Some state judges are elected to defined terms; others are appointed to terms by the governor;

3. 358 U.S. 1 (1958).
4. *The Federalist* No. 78 (Clinton Rossiter ed. 2003) (Alexander Hamilton): 402.

still others are initially appointed by the governor but must stand for a retention election. The states exhibit—both among themselves and, sometimes, even within a single state—wide variation in judicial selection.

8. States also supply their own procedures for their courts. States need not follow the same procedures that federal courts do, and no state has adopted exactly the same procedures as federal courts, but most states use federal procedures as a model. State courts have the final authority to interpret both state procedural law and state substantive law.

9. Although states operate in a sovereign capacity, they are subservient to federal law. The Constitution imposes some specific limits on states—they cannot declare war or coin their own money, for example. In addition, the Supremacy Clause makes federal law the supreme law of the land in all states. Under this provision, states must abide by federal law, and state law must yield to conflicting federal law. Congress has long allowed state courts to adjudicate questions of federal law, but it also has given the Supreme Court appellate jurisdiction to review decisions of state courts that do so.[5]

IV. The Role of Civil Litigation in U.S. Society

10. American litigation serves more than the function of dispute resolution. It also serves the function of law pronouncement under the courts' broad and authoritative interpretative power. The power of law pronouncement means that the courts are often sought out to provide the authoritative answer on the meaning of laws that affect the more important policies of U.S. society. Law pronouncement has, in turn, a profound regulatory effect on primary actors. Reliance on this regulatory effect offsets the need for *ex ante* regulation through the bureaucratic state. Congress need not investigate workplace discrimination, for example, because it can rely on the courts—hearing claims of unlawful workplace discrimination initiated by private employees—to decide when the law has been violated and to order relief for any violations. Thus, a critical function of American courts is to provide indirect enforcement of the laws.

11. American litigation is also party-driven and adversarial. American focus on individualism and skepticism of government lead to a litigation system in which the judge usually declines to act on their own and instead waits until a party asks the judge to decide an issue in dispute. Exceptions to this practice exist, and the trend of American judges is to take a more active managerial role in overseeing cases, but passivity remains the general norm.

5. 28 U.S.C. §1257.

§2. Delimitation of the Subject Matter

I. Definition of Civil Procedure

12. Within American law, civil procedure consists of the rules governing the pursuit of civil disputes for court adjudication, including forum selection, pleadings, service, joinder of claims and parties, discovery, motions, preliminary relief, trial, preclusion, and judgment enforcement.

II. Distinction from Other Types of Procedure

13. The federal structure of government means that, at least since 1938, the procedure in federal court generally follows federal laws of procedure, while the procedure in state court generally follows state laws. Each state has its own procedures. For various historical and practical reasons, American legal education tends to focus on federal procedure, with only modest attention given to state procedure. Practicing attorneys generally know federal procedure, as well as the procedure in their state of practice, but they generally are unknowledgable of other states' procedures. The international community, too, tends to look to federal procedure as emblematic of American civil litigation. For those reasons, this volume focuses on federal procedure, with occasional discussion of state procedure where applicable or of interest.

14. The prosecution of crimes by state or federal prosecutors is universally subject to a separate and distinct system of criminal procedure, which often reflects intricate state and federal constitutional provisions that give individuals extraordinary protection against the loss of liberty by conviction of a crime. Criminal matters typically seek punitive relief imposed reflecting governmental or moral opprobrium. Civil matters, by contrast, are typically private disputes (though the dispute may still arise with a governmental entity, such as for violations of civil rights, employment disputes involving governmental employees, and the like) for money or injunctive relief. This volume focuses solely on civil procedure.

15. The constitutional limits on federal governmental power constrain the federal courts. These constraints often fall under the terminology of court "jursidiction," but the theoretical sources of those limits are grounded in constitutionally structural notions of federalism and the separation of powers. Those issues also commonly bridge the civil-criminal divide. For those reasons, issues of federal judicial power under the Constitution are relegated to a separate body of doctrines categorized under the moniker of Federal Courts.

16. The vast array of regulatory agencies created by state and federal law operates under generally autonomous rules of administrative procedure established both by congressional acts and by the agencies themselves.[6] The procedures and authorities for agency adjudication are not generally conceptualized as civil procedure but instead are encapsulated within the separate field of administrative law.

17. The procedures for appellate practice, habeas corpus, and bankruptcy contain specialized rules of procedure devoted to the peculiarities of those fields. This volume covers the general field of federal civil procedure, not those specialized areas.

18. Alternative forums for civil adjudication exist, including private tribunals like arbitration. This volume does not address alternative dispute resolution in detail but does, in Part IV, offer a brief overview of some of the major forms of ADR seen in civil disputes in Part 4.

§3. Sources of Procedural Law

19. Matters of jurisdiction and forum selection in the federal district courts are set primarily by the Constitution, federal statute, and Rule 4 of the Federal Rules of Civil Procedure. Rules of preclusion, also known as res judicata, are primarily set by federal common law. The pursuit and adjudication of claims and defenses are governed primarily by the Federal Rules of Civil Procedure. Each of these sources of law is given additional content and meaning by the federal courts in the tradition of the common law.

§4. General Features of the Administration of Civil Justice

I. Characteristics of Civil Procedure

20. The American system of civil procedure is primarily an adversarial one, in which parties with opposing interests vie to persuade the judge and the trier of fact as to the merits of their conflicting contentions of law and fact. Typically, the American system relies on the parties to present their case as they see fit, with the judge remaining passive until called upon, by motion or trial, to adjudicate any disputes presented by the parties. This principle of party presentation, though not inexorable, dominates American litigation culture.

21. Some key exceptions to this principle exist. Although most questions of forum selection are left to the parties, the federal courts have an independent obligation to assure themselves of their own subject-matter jurisdiction to hear a case.[7] Class actions, as representative litigation, require judicial scrutiny of procedural requirements.[8] Matters of equity, including forms of equitable relief, remain within

6. Administrative Procedure Act, 5 U.S.C. §§500,et seq.
7. *Insurance Corp. of Ireland v. Compagnie des Bauxites de Guinee*, 456 U.S. 694 (1982): 454.
8. FRCP 23.

the independent control of the courts, as do matters committed to inherent judicial power, such as sanctions, court decorum, and the doctrine of *forum non conveniens*. Finally, a significant countercurrent to the principle of party presentation is the trend among federal judges, encouraged by the Federal Rules of Civil Procedure, to exercise more supervisory and managerial authority over pretrial matters in certain kinds of cases.[9]

22. Federal civil procedure is transsubstantive, meaning that uniform rules apply to a case irrespective of its subject matter, parties, or relief sought. The federal courts have no small-claims procedure; a case for statutory penalties of USD 500 for telemarketing calls unlawful under the Telephone Consumer Protection Act[10] is subject to the same rules as a complex, multibillion-dollar case against an oil company for an oil spill. Likewise, though much of American civil litigation resolves purely private disputes, such as breaches of contracts, localized torts, and property trespasses, the system also resolves cases of broad public interest, such as consumer rights and safety, employment discrimination and safety, civil rights against governmental intrusion, antitrust compliance, and environmental regulation. The impact of such "public-law litigation" extends far beyond the clash of the personal interests of the particular (often nominal) litigants. Although a slip-and-fall case and a suit to challenge the legality of racially segregated public schools have very different public effects, they are both subject to the same rules of civil procedure.

23. Though transsubstantive, federal civil procedure often applies flexibly to the needs of the case by giving the judge broad discretion over the process and by relying on the principle of party presentation. For example, the Federal Rules of Civil Procedure set a presumptive limit of ten depositions for each party, but that limit can be narrowed or expanded by court order or party stipulation.[11] The vehicles of flexibility and discretion enable transsubstantive rules to be tailored, through implementation, to the needs of the case.

II. Fundamental Guarantees

24. The principle of due process of law guaranteed by the Fifth Amendment to the Constitution encompasses fair notice, fair opportunity to be heard, fair procedures, and impartial adjudication. The First Amendment also protects the right of court access, including by members of the media and general public, as well as the freedom of speech, though those rights may be tempered by the need for effective and efficient court adjudication.[12]

9. FRCP 16.
10. 47 U.S.C. §227(b).
11. FRCP 30(a)(2).
12. *Berner v. Delahanty*, 129 F.3d 20 (1st Cir. 1997).

25. The Seventh Amendment preserves the right to jury trial in civil cases at common law, where more than USD 20 is at stake. The federal courts have construed the scope of this right by reference to British jury trial practice in 1791, the date of ratification of the Seventh Amendment.

26. Appeal is widely valued and liberally exercised in American civil litigation but is a privilege extended by tradition rather than by constitutional mandate. It is generally recognized that there should be at least one level of appeal of decisions made by a judge in the first instance, but it has never been held that the unavailability of appeal in a particular case conflicts with the federal constitutional guarantee of due process of law. In the federal system, appeal is permitted as of right from all final judgments by trial courts, with most interlocutory orders subject to earlier review only in exceptional circumstances.[13]

13. 28 U.S.C. §§1291–1292.

Part I. Judicial Structure and Jurisdiction

Chapter 1. The Courts and Their Members

§1. Court Structures

27. The Constitution mandates the existence of the Supreme Court but leaves the creation of all lower federal courts to Congress.[14] Congress has created both trial courts and intermediate courts of appeal. The three-level organization can be conceptualized as a triangle. At the base of the triangle are numerous trial courts (usually called "district courts"). The middle of the triangle represents thirteen courts of appeal, organized into "circuits." At the apex of the triangle resides the Supreme Court.

28. Congress has created nearly a hundred district courts. Each state has one to four district courts, depending upon state population. The number of judges of each federal district court varies from two to more than twenty judges, depending upon district population.

29. Congress has established thirteen intermediate courts of appeals. With the exception of the Court of Appeals for the Federal Circuit, which has nationwide appellate jurisdiction over patent cases and certain other special appeals, each Court of Appeals hears civil and criminal cases appealed from the district courts within the geographic region covered by the circuit. The courts of appeals vary in terms of area, population, and number of judges. The Court of Appeals for the First Circuit, for example, consists of six circuit judges and hears cases appealed from the district courts in Maine, Massachusetts, New Hampshire, Puerto Rico, and Rhode Island. The Court of Appeals for the Ninth Circuit consists of twenty-nine circuit judges and hears cases appealed from the district courts in Alaska, Arizona, California, Hawaii, Idaho, Montana, Nevada, Oregon, Washington, Guam, and the Northern Mariana Islands. The Court of Appeals for the District of Columbia Circuit hears cases that originate in Washington, DC or in certain administrative agencies. The courts of appeals generally review issues of law de novo, issues of fact for clear error, and discretionary decisions for abuse of discretion.

14. U.S. Const. Art. III, §1.

30. The Supreme Court has jurisdiction to review decisions of all the federal courts of appeals.[15] Additionally, the Supreme Court has the power to review the decisions of the highest state court in any state when the decision turns on a question of federal law.[16] The Supreme Court's appellate jurisdiction is almost entirely discretionary. With rare exceptions, it can pick and choose which cases appealed from the federal courts of appeals or from state courts that it wants to hear. Currently, the Supreme Court has nine judges: a Chief Justice and eight Associate Justices.

31. Each of the fifty states is free to organize its courts as it sees fit. Generally, however, the states have a triangle structure similar to the federal system: a set of trial courts of general jurisdiction, a few intermediate courts of appeals, and a supreme court of last resort. State-court systems are more likely than the federal-court system to have specialized courts, such as family courts, small-claims courts, and others.

§2. Selection of Judges

32. The Constitution gives the President the power to appoint all federal judges, with the advice and consent of the Senate.[17] Once confirmed, federal judges enjoy lifetime tenure, subject only to removal by impeachment, and their salaries may not be diminished while in office.[18] These provisions are designed to insulate federal judges from political pressures.

33. In addition to district judges appointed under the Constitution, the district courts often employ magistrate judges, civil employees hired by the district court to assist in managing cases. Magistrate judges serve only for a fixed term of years. Magistrate judges are particularly helpful in resolving pretrial disputes between the parties and other procedural matters concerning, among other things, the civil discovery process.

34. The Constitution sets no qualifications for appointment as a federal judge, but, in practice, federal judges tend to be selected from among the brightest legal minds and with significant relevant experience.

35. The method of selecting state judges varies from state to state. Some state judges are elected to terms; others are appointed to terms. Few state judges are appointed with life tenure.

---

15. 28 U.S.C. §2107.
16. 28 U.S.C. §1257.
17. U.S. Const. Art. II, §2, cl. 2.
18. U.S. Const. Art. III, §1.

Chapter 2. The Bar

§1. Conditions for Admission

36. Each state requires state-approved admission to that state's bar to practice law in the state or appear before the state courts in that state. Admission requirements vary but generally require graduation from an approved law school and passage of a state-administered bar exam. With very few exceptions, the bar exams are generalist exams; passage enables practice in any area of the law, including criminal practice. Remaining in good standing with the bar generally requires an annual payment of dues and annual compliance with minimum hours of continuing legal education (CLE). Federal courts ordinarily admit applicants who are members in good standing of the bar of the highest court of the state in which the federal court exists.

37. State and federal courts routinely allow a member in good standing of a different state's bar to appear before them for a specific case using a procedure called *pro hac vice*. The practice is widespread and routine: the applicant files a motion, with supporting documentation showing the applicant's good standing with another bar, and the court grants the motion to enable the applicant to appear. Some courts will require, as a condition of admission, the applicant to partner with an attorney barred in the forum state during the pendency of the case.

§2. Discipline and Regulation

38. Courts, agencies, and private organizations all regulate the legal profession. Courts have the inherent power to control proceedings in their courtroom, which necessarily entails the ability to regulate attorneys who appear—or try to appear—before them.[19] Court sanctions, including fines and other penalties, help deter violations of court decorum, good-faith representations, and court rules of conduct.

39. A designated state agency or the state Supreme Court—whichever body regulates the legal profession more generally in a particular state—promulgates or adopts codes of conduct and ethics that govern the practice of law in that state, often modeled on the Model Rules of Professional Conduct promulgated by the American Bar Association, a highly respected, private, nationwide association of the legal profession. Conduct and ethics rules commonly cover matters such as the handling of client funds, client confidentiality, conflicts of interest, and the tension between the duties of candor owed to the court and the duties of zealous representation owed to the client. Violations can result in warnings, suspensions, or disbarment.

19. *Ex Parte Wall*, 107 U.S. 265 (1882).

Part II. Jurisdiction

Chapter 1. Domestic Jurisdiction

§1. Subject-Matter Jurisdiction

I. Principles

40. Subject-matter divisions allocate a particular kind of case to a particular court or set of courts. Within the federal-court system, subject-matter divisions are rare. Certain bankruptcy matters, tax matters, administrative matters, patent matters, and matters involving tort suits against the federal government are committed to specific tribunals. But, in the main, federal courts are generalist courts, not specialized courts. State courts exhibit more specialization; many state-court systems have specialized family courts, criminal courts, small-claims courts, and the like.

41. Federal-court subject-matter jurisdiction tends to focus not on allocations within the federal system but on the allocation of a case to either state court or federal court. Federal courts can hear only those cases authorized by both the Constitution and federal statute. If a case cannot be heard in federal court, state courts generally are available to hear the case in the first instance; if the case involves a federal issue, the Supreme Court can hear an appeal from the state-court system.

42. Because of the longstanding historical deference to state-court authority, when Congress gives the federal courts subject-matter jurisdiction, it usually does not disturb the state courts' concurrent jurisdiction to hear the case (again, subject to appeal to the U.S. Supreme Court). In a few areas, such as antitrust, patent, copyright, and securities law, Congress has given the federal courts exclusive jurisdiction and deprived the state courts of concurrent jurisdiction. But, for most claims eligible for federal-court jurisdiction, the plaintiff can choose to file in either state or federal court.

43. Defects in federal subject-matter jurisdiction, whether constitutional or statutory, cannot be waived or forfeited by the parties; defects can be raised at any time, including for the first time on appeal; the parties cannot consent or stipulate to federal-court jurisdiction when jurisdiction is otherwise lacking; and a federal court always has an independent obligation to assure itself of its own subject-matter jurisdiction. A court without subject-matter jurisdiction has no power to proceed except to dismiss the case.

44. Article III of the Constitution extends federal-court jurisdiction:

> to all cases, in law and equity, arising under this Constitution, the laws of the United States, and treaties made, or which shall be made, under their authority;—to all cases affecting ambassadors, other public ministers and consuls;—to all cases of admiralty and maritime jurisdiction;—to controversies to which the United States shall be a party;—to controversies between two or more states;—between a state and citizens of another state—between citizens of different states;—between citizens of the same state claiming lands under grants of different states, and between a state, or the citizens thereof, and foreign states, citizens or subjects.[20]

45. This constitutional grant of power is not self-executing. It leaves to Congress how much—if any—to grant to which federal courts. The Constitution does specifically limit the Supreme Court's original jurisdiction to only "cases affecting ambassadors, other public ministers and consuls, and those in which a state shall be party,"[21] and Congress cannot give the Supreme Court original jurisdiction in other kinds of cases.[22] But the Constitution leaves to Congress all other authority for allocating cases within the constitutional grant to whichever courts Congress wishes.

46. Today, the most important grants of federal subject-matter jurisdiction are: (1) federal-question cases ("cases, in law and equity, arising under this Constitution, the laws of the United States, and treaties made, or which shall be made, under their authority") and (2) diversity-jurisdiction cases ("between citizens of different states … and between a state, or the citizens thereof, and foreign states, citizens or subjects").

47. In the famous case *Cohens v. Virginia*, the Supreme Court announced: "We have no more right to decline the exercise of jurisdiction which is given than to usurp that which is not given."[23] That statement has never been taken literally; various judicially created doctrines of abstention have allowed federal courts to decline to exercise subject-matter jurisdiction granted to them by the Constitution and by Congress,[24] and courts retain the inherent power to decline to hear a case on the ground of *forum non conveniens*.[25] But those doctrines are narrowly applied, such that unless Congress expressly gives a court discretion over its own subject-matter jurisdiction, federal courts have a "virtually unflagging obligation"[26] to exercise jurisdiction when properly granted by Congress and invoked by a party.

20. U.S. Const. Art. III, §2.
21. *Ibid.*
22. *Marbury v. Madison*, 5 U.S. (1 Cranch) 137 (1803).
23. 19 U.S. (6 Wheat.) 264, 404 (1821).
24. *Sprint Communications, Inc. v. Jacobs*, 571 U.S. 69 (2013).
25. *Gulf Oil Corp. v. Gilbert*, 330 U.S. 501 (1947).
26. *Colorado River Water Conservation District v. United States*, 424 U.S. 800, 817 (1976).

II. Federal-Question Jurisdiction

48. The Supreme Court, in the famous case of *Osborn v. Bank of the United States*, held that a case qualifies for the constitutional grant of federal-question jurisdiction when it contains an essential federal ingredient.[27] There, auditors of the state of Ohio taxed, as provided under state law, a branch of the Bank of the United States located in Ohio. The state law was unconstitutional under a previous ruling, *McCulloch v. Maryland*,[28] so the Bank sued the auditors for return of the confiscated funds. No federal law provided a cause of action for the relief sought, but Ohio state law did. Nevertheless, the Bank chose to sue the auditors in federal district court in Ohio. The auditors argued that the federal court lacked subject-matter jurisdiction because the cause of action was created only by state law. The Supreme Court disagreed and held that the case arose under federal law because the sue was brought by the Bank, which was an entity created entirely by federal law and could only sue at all because of the congressional act authorizing the Bank to sue. Even though the Bank's statutory creation and authorization to sue were not contested, they amounted to an essential federal ingredient that necessarily caused the Bank's suit to arise under federal law for purposes of constitutional subject-matter jurisdiction.

49. Such a broad scope of constitutionally authorized federal-question jurisdiction could, if extended to the federal district courts by Congress, dramatically shift the allocation of cases, including many cases with prominent state-law claims and issues, into federal court. But Congress did not grant the lower federal courts general federal-question jurisdiction until 1875. Until then, most federal claims were brought in state court, with appellate jurisdiction ultimately in the U.S. Supreme Court.

50. The energization of federal power and the expansion of interstate commerce after the Civil War refocused the importance of federal-court jurisdiction to hear and decide federal cases. In 1875, Congress statutorily granted federal district courts federal-question jurisdiction in language that persists today: over "civil actions arising under" federal law.[29] This grant of subject-matter jurisdiction to the federal district courts is concurrent; state courts continue to have equivalent subject-matter jurisdiction to hear the same cases.

51. The statutory language clearly allows federal courts to hear federal claims. But it also potentially allows them to hear state claims that contain, in *Osborn*'s terminology, an essential federal ingredient. Although the statutory language uses the same terminology ("arising under") as the Constitution, the Supreme Court has construed the statutory grant as narrower than the *Osborn* test for constitutional federal-question jurisdiction. In *Louisville & Nashville Railroad Co. v. Mottley*, the Supreme Court held that a case only arises under federal law for purposes of the

27. 22 U.S. (9 Wheat.) 738 (1824).
28. 17 U.S. (4 Wheat.) 316 (1819).
29. 28 U.S.C. §1331.

statutory grant when the federal ingredient is part of the "well-pleaded complaint."[30] In that case, the Mottleys were given free railroad passes by a railroad as settlement of a previous lawsuit. Congress, however, then passed a statute making those passes unlawful, so the railroad refused to honor them. The Mottleys sued the railroad in federal court for breach of contract, a state-law cause of action. But in the complaint, the Mottleys alleged that the railroad would assert a defense to contract liability based on the federal statute. The Mottleys further argued that the statute was unconstitutional under the U.S. Constitution. Both issues were federal ingredients in the case; indeed, the only issues disputed in the case were those federal issues. Nevertheless, the Supreme Court held that the case did not arise under federal law under the statute because the statute required the federal ingredient to be part of the plaintiff's affirmative claim for relief rather than part of a defense or a counterclaim asserted by the defendant. Federal defenses commonly arise in slander and libel cases: state-law causes of action are limited by the restrictions of freedom of speech in the First Amendment, which can be asserted by way of a defense. Such cases are not eligible for federal-question jurisdiction under the statute.

52. The *Mottley* rule restricts most federal-question cases to cases involving federal claims and federal relief. But some state-law claims do contain a federal ingredient that would meet the *Mottley* test, and so the Supreme Court has imposed another test for state-law claims with embedded federal issues. In *Grable & Sons Metal Products, Inc. v. Darue Engineering & Manufacturing, Inc.*, the Internal Revenue Service (IRS) foreclosed on a piece of property owned by Grable & Sons to satisfy a delinquent tax liability. At the foreclosure sale, Darue purchased the property. Grable subsequently sued Darue for quiet title, arguing that because the IRS failed to provide proper notice of the sale under federal law, the tax sale was invalid. Although the cause of action was created solely by state law, the only dispute was whether the IRS notice was proper under federal law. If so, Darue owned the property. If not, Grable owned the property. The federal issue was an essential part of Grable's well-pleaded complaint because it was part of its affirmative claim for relief, which Grable could not prove entitlement to without proving the lawlessness of the notice. The Supreme Court held that such state-law claims with embedded federal issues *could* arise under federal law for purposes of the statutory grant of federal-question jurisdiction, and it set out a four-part test. First, the federal issue must be necessarily raised by the plaintiff's claim. Second, the federal issue must be actually disputed by the parties. Third, the federal issue must be of substantial importance to the federal system to warrant federal-court experience, solicitude, and uniformity. Fourth, the allocation of such claims to federal courts must not disrupt the congressional division of authority between state and federal courts. The Supreme Court held all four factors met. The lawfulness of the IRS's notice was both necessary to Grable's claim and actually disputed by Darue. How the IRS should provide notice of tax sales was of substantial interest to the federal system because the IRS must have certain, predictable, and uniform rules for the efficient and effective collection of tax revenue. And because the case involved a pure issue

30. 211 U.S. 149 (1908).

of law, the Supreme Court's resolution of the issue would provide clarity sufficient to stave off future lawsuits over the issue in federal court.

53. The Supreme Court also has held that the pleading of a state-law claim that has been completely preempted by federal law necessarily raises only a federal claim and thus arises under federal law for purposes of statutory federal-question jurisdiction. Although the lower courts have applied the "complete preemption" doctrine more broadly, the Supreme Court has given this sweeping construction to only three federal statutes: §301 of the Labor-Management Relations Act, §502 of the Employees Retirement Income Security Act, and §86 of the National Bank Act.[31] Any lawsuit seeking to enforce the rights these statutes create is a suit that arises under federal law, even if the plaintiff by "artful pleading" seeks to characterize the suit as one to enforce only parallel rights under state law because these statutes displace state law and leave only federal rights for enforcement.

54. A lawsuit filed under the Declaratory Judgment Act—which authorizes any party to sue for a declaratory judgment on a particular issue involved in a claim—does not itself necessarily arise under federal law. Rather, the lawsuit arises under federal law only if the underlying affirmative claim would arise under federal law.[32]

III. Diversity and Alienage Jurisdiction

A. Principles

55. Suits between citizens of different states or between a citizen of a state and citizen of another country present the risk that the courts of a state may favor that state's citizens over other states' or countries' citizens. Consider, for example, Wal-Mart, which is headquartered in the state of Arkansas and has a prominent presence there. It employs many Arkansas citizens, donates money to Arkansas arts and public works, and generates substantial tax revenue for the state. Say Wal-Mart enters into a USD 2 billion contract with a California technology company to purchase and use that company's inventory-management software. But Wal-Mart then breaches the contract, and the California company sues Wal-Mart for USD 1 billion in damages. The California plaintiff may be wary about suing in an Arkansas state court. After all, if the California plaintiff prevails, a large amount of Wal-Mart's money will leave Arkansas for California, perhaps making it more difficult for Wal-Mart to use those funds to benefit Arkansas, its citizens, and its officials. Arkansas judges are elected, and perhaps Wal-Mart regularly donates to judicial candidates who have decided cases favorable to Wal-Mart's interests in the past. For those reasons, the California plaintiff may worry that Arkansas judges and juries are likely to favor

31. *Beneficial National Bank v. Anderson*, 539 U.S. 1 (2003).
32. *Franchise Tax Board v. Construction Laborers Vacation Trust*, 463 U.S. 1 (1983); *Skelly Oil Co. v. Phillips Petroleum Co.*, 339 U.S. 667 (1950).

Wal-Mart in the dispute. At the very least, if the Arkansas court does decide the case in Wal-Mart's favor, observers might wonder if in-state favoritism played a role.

B. Constitutional Diversity and Alienage Jurisdiction

56. The Framers of the U.S. Constitution worried about this, too. They provided, in the Constitution, for federal courts to have jurisdiction over such cases. Federal judges are appointed for life by national officials, not elected by a single state's citizens or appointed by state officials, and therefore federal judges are seen as providing a forum less likely to be swayed by in-state biases. Charges of bias are serious, though, and so the Framers were cautious to pitch the concern as one of the *perception* of bias rather than of actual bias. In addition, some scholars and judges have argued that other motivations were at play, including the need for federal courts to have some cases to adjudicate and the need to prioritize national economic development over local economic development.

57. No matter the actual reason, constitutional diversity jurisdiction was adopted and, today, is widely justified as a protection against the perception of in-state bias. The Constitution grants federal courts jurisdiction over cases—primarily state-law cases—between citizens of different states and between citizens of a state and citizens of a foreign state. The latter provision was justified both on state-bias grounds and on the propriety of having a national court decide matters with international dimensions. The Constitution does not, however, grant federal-court jurisdiction over state-law cases involving only foreign parties.

58. The Constitution extends diversity jurisdiction if any plaintiff is of a different state or national citizenship from any defendant.[33] Such diversity is called "minimal diversity." The Constitution imposes no amount-in-controversy requirement for diversity or alienage jurisdiction.

C. Statutory Diversity and Alienage Jurisdiction

1. Minimal and Complete Diversity

59. Congress has authorized the federal district courts to hear suits on the basis of minimal diversity—when any plaintiff's citizenship is different from any defendant's—only in three special contexts: when the suit involves the "interpleader" of rival claimants to the same property,[34] suits under the Multiparty,

33. *State Farm & Casualty Co. v. Tashire*, 386 U.S. 523 (1967).
34. 28 U.S.C. §1335.

Multiforum Trial Jurisdiction Act of 2002,[35] and suits under the Class Action Fairness Act of 2005.[36]

60. Under the general diversity statute, 28 U.S.C. §1332, however, the federal district courts lack jurisdiction unless "complete diversity" exists.[37] This means that if any plaintiff and any defendant are citizens of the same state, federal diversity jurisdiction is lacking. Thus, the statute does not authorize federal diversity jurisdiction over a lawsuit by a California plaintiff and a Nevada plaintiff against a Nevada defendant and a New York defendant.

61. For cases founded solely on alienage jurisdiction, if any plaintiff and any defendant are foreign nationals—regardless of their specific nationality—alienage jurisdiction is lacking. Thus, the statute does not authorize alienage jurisdiction over a lawsuit by a California plaintiff and a French plaintiff against a German defendant. In addition, the statute eliminates alienage jurisdiction if any foreign party is a lawful permanent resident of the United States and is domiciled in the same state as an opponent. Thus, a California plaintiff can sue a French defendant in federal court under alienage jurisdiction unless the French defendant is a lawful permanent resident of the United States domiciled in California.

62. Federal courts are not bound to accept cases as structured by plaintiffs. The doctrine of "fraudulent joinder" requires that the federal court determine its jurisdiction without regard to parties joined by a legally insubstantial claim.

2. Citizenship

63. The state citizenship of a natural person, for purposes of diversity jurisdiction, is based on "domicile," the person's true, permanent, and fixed residence. A person's domicile is their place of birth unless changed to a new domicile by having, concurrently, both a physical presence in a new state and a subjective intent to reside in that new state indefinitely.[38] Once that test is met, the person is a domiciliary of the new state for diversity-jurisdiction purposes, until establishing a new domicile through satisfaction of the same test. Importantly, this test is different from mere residence. Thus, a lifelong resident of California who goes to boarding school in New York is not a New York domiciliary for diversity-jurisdiction purposes unless the person has formed a subjective intent to reside in New York indefinitely, even if the person has been in residence at the school for several consecutive years. Recognizing that subjective intent can be easily manipulated, courts often credit

---

35. 28 U.S.C. §§1369, 1441(e). The Act deals with mass torts in which at least seventy-five people have died at a single location, permitting resulting litigation to be commenced in or removed to federal court unless the mass tort is essentially localized, involving events in and parties from only one state.
36. 28 U.S.C. §1332(d).
37. *Strawbridge v. Curtiss*, 7 U.S. (3 Cranch) 267 (1806).
38. *Mas v. Perry*, 492 F.2d 1242 (5th Cir. 1974).

objective indices of permanent domicile, such as the purchase of a fixed primary residence in the state, the registration of a car or the right to vote in the state, and the like.

64. An unincorporated legal entity with the capacity to sue or be sued in its own name, such as a partnership, association, labor union, and limited-liability corporation, is a citizen of every state that its members are citizens.[39] Its state of organization and principal place of business are irrelevant. Thus, a law firm organized under the laws of New York with its headquarters in New York but with partners only from New Jersey and Connecticut is a citizen, for diversity-jurisdiction purposes, of New Jersey and Connecticut but not of New York. Entities with many widely dispersed members may be citizens of many states. If any one of those citizenships is common with a party opponent, complete diversity is lacking. For that reason, establishing diversity jurisdiction may be difficult when the case involves a large unincorporated entity.

65. A corporation's citizenship, for diversity-jurisdiction purposes, is not determined by the members test but instead is defined by statute as both its state of incorporation and the state where its principal place of business is located.[40] The Supreme Court has determined that a corporation's principal place of business is where the high-ranking officers direct the corporation's operations, which normally will be its headquarters offices.[41] A corporation can have only one state with its principal place of business, which, in difficult or unusual circumstances, such as for a corporation with multiple headquarters, the federal court must identify.

66. A party's citizenship for purposes of a particular lawsuit's eligibility for diversity jurisdiction is deemed fixed as of the time diversity jurisdiction is invoked.[42] Thus, a California domiciliary who sues a Delaware corporation with its principal place of business in New York cannot, mid-case, suddenly destroy diversity jurisdiction by establishing a new domicile in New York. Any new lawsuits in federal court after that change in domicile, however, will consider the person a citizen of New York. Thus, a party can be a citizen of one state for one case and a citizen of another state for another case.

3. Amount in Controversy

67. In addition to requiring complete diversity of citizenship, the statutory grant of diversity and alienage jurisdiction requires a sufficient amount in controversy. (No jurisdictional amount is required for federal-question or admiralty jurisdiction.) The statute requires that the amount in controversy exceed USD 75,000, exclusive

39. *Americold Realty Trust v. ConAgra Foods, Inc.*, 577 U.S. 378 (2016).
40. 28 U.S.C. §1332(c).
41. *Hertz Corp. v. Friend*, 559 U.S. 77 (2010).
42. *Grupo Dataflux v. Atlas Global Group, L.P.*, 541 U.S. 567 (2003).

of interest added to the judgment and exclusive of the costs of suit.[43] One rationale of the amount-in-controversy requirement is that it helps ensure that only significant cases—in which in-state bias is mostly likely to be perceived—are granted federal-court jurisdiction, thereby vindicating the purpose of diversity jurisdiction without flooding the federal courts' dockets with insubstantial state-law cases.

68. In a suit by a single plaintiff against a single defendant, the total amount claimed "in good faith" by the plaintiff is the measure of the amount in controversy, unless the law prevents recovery exceeding the jurisdictional threshold to a legal certainty.[44] For example, a plaintiff who seeks damages for personal injuries and is entitled by law to recover noneconomic damages for "pain and suffering" incident to the injury can easily claim damages in excess of USD 75,000 threshold for diversity jurisdiction. But if law caps noneconomic damages at a maximum of two times the economic damage, and if the plaintiff seeks USD 100,000 in noneconomic damages but just USD 20,000 in economic damages, then it is a legal certainty that the plaintiff cannot recover more than USD 75,000. The "legal certainty" rule has important ramifications in cases in which punitive damages are legally recoverable. Even a plaintiff who has suffered only slight personal injury can easily claim sufficient punitive damages in excess of the jurisdictional threshold unless the law caps the punitive damages at a lower amount.

69. Because the statutory limit is phrased in terms of dollars, nonmonetary relief—such as an injunction—must be converted into dollars to determine whether the amount-in-controversy threshold has been exceeded. The diversity statute provides no guidance on how to value such controversies. In *Mississippi & Missouri Railroad Co. v. Ward*, the Supreme Court merely restated the problem by declaring that "the value of the object" must govern the determination of the amount in controversy.[45] In that case, the alleged nuisance of the defendant's railroad-bridge piers across the Mississippi River impeded the plaintiff's riverboat business, and the plaintiff sought abatement of the nuisance. It was obvious that the cost of removing or relocating the bridge would exceed the required amount, but it was not obvious that the value of the plaintiff's business, or at least of its diminution in value should the plaintiff's suit be unsuccessful, would exceed that amount. In upholding diversity jurisdiction, the Supreme Court failed to specify just which of these calculations it had in mind as "the value of the object" of the litigation. The general rule followed by the lower courts is that specific relief may be valued from either party's perspective, as measured either by the loss to the plaintiff in the absence of relief or by the cost to the defendant should the requested relief be granted.

70. One claimant can aggregate the value of all claims that claimant has against a single defendant, and the aggregated value will be the measure of each claim's satisfaction of the amount-in-controversy requirement. Thus, if a plaintiff asserts a tort claim for USD 50,000 in personal injuries and a contract claim for USD 50,000

43. 28 U.S.C. § 1332(a).
44. *St. Paul Mercury Indemnity Co. v. Red Cab Co.*, 303 U.S. 283 (1938).
45. 67 U.S. 485 (1862).

for commercial damages against a single defendant, the separate damages for each can be aggregated, and each claim will exceed the statutory amount-in-controversy threshold. This aggregation rule applies even if the two claims are unrelated to each other. However, aggregation across other claims or across parties has traditionally been permitted only when the right or liability at issue is "joint" rather than "several."

IV. Supplemental Jurisdiction

71. Supplemental jurisdiction allows a federal court to hear a nondiverse state-law claim when joined with a claim eligible for diversity or federal-question jurisdiction. Civil lawsuits today commonly feature multiple claims. If at least one of the claims is eligible for diversity, alienage, or federal-question jurisdiction and at least one of the claims is ineligible, three options exist. The first is for the eligible claims to be heard by a federal court and the ineligible claims to be heard by a state court. That option makes sense if the claims are unrelated because each claim is allocated to the "right" court, and joinder would produce no litigation efficiencies. But if the claims are so related that litigating them in separate courts could produce great inefficiencies or risk inconsistent judgments, then two other options arise: join them in a single state-court case or join them in a single federal-court case. Joinder in state court is almost always a legal option because state courts generally have concurrent jurisdiction over claims eligible for federal-court jurisdiction, but it is not always a good practical option. For one, state-court joinder could undermine the systemic benefit of encouraging federal courts to hear federal-question cases. For another, additional federal-ineligible claims could be added late to a lawsuit originally filed with only federal-eligible claims. The third option—joinder in federal court—would be useful in such situations.

72. Prior to 1990, the federal courts developed doctrines called "pendent jurisdiction" and "ancillary jurisdiction" to accommodate this third option. The famous case of *United Mine Workers v. Gibbs* found constitutional authorization for such a practice because the constitutional grant covers the entire "case" or "controversy," not just specific claims.[46] As long as one claim in the case is eligible for federal subject-matter jurisdiction, reasoned the Court, then all other claims that form "a common nucleus of operative fact" can be heard in federal court as a single "case" or "controversy."[47] The Court deemed federal-court jurisdiction over the otherwise-ineligible claims to be discretionary, however, and counseled dismissal of such claims if they dominated the case or if all federal-eligible claims had been dismissed.[48]

73. One problem with the third option is that it requires a misallocation of a state-law claim to federal court when the only justification for having a federal court

46. 383 U.S. 715 (1966).
47. *Ibid.*, at 725.
48. *Ibid.*, at 726.

hear that claim is efficiency based on the relatedness of the state-law claim to other joined claims within federal subject-matter jurisdiction. The downsides of having a federal court hear a state-law claim not eligible for diversity jurisdiction are that: (1) adjudicating the claim requires federal-court resources, (2) state courts are deprived of the opportunity to exercise sovereign authority over claims more appropriately within their jurisdiction, (3) federal-court adjudication will not contribute to the development of authoritative precedent on state law, and (4) federal courts are presumably less expert at adjudicating state-law claims, so efficiency and accuracy of adjudication may be lower in federal court than in state court. *Gibbs* arguably took these factors into account when giving guidance about how federal courts should exercise their discretion in hearing such claims.

74. Another problem with the third option is that parties might try to use it to get around the statutory rule of complete diversity in diversity cases. Say, for example, a California plaintiff would like to sue a California defendant and a Nevada defendant in federal court on related state-law claims. The plaintiff generally cannot do so under either federal-question jurisdiction or diversity jurisdiction. But if the plaintiff first sues only the Nevada defendant in federal court based on diversity jurisdiction, then, later, the plaintiff could add the California defendant and argue that the federal court should hear that claim too, for efficiency reasons, under the third option. In other words, the third option would allow the plaintiff to circumvent the rule of complete diversity. In *Owen Equipment & Erection Co. v. Kroger*, the Supreme Court confronted this problem and held that, in such circumstances, federal courts lacked subject-matter jurisdiction to hear otherwise ineligible claims that would subvert the rule of complete diversity.[49]

75. Yet another problem with the third option is that, prior to 1990, it arguably lacked statutory authorization. The federal-question statute and the diversity statute both extend jurisdiction over "civil actions." If a state claim falls outside of the "civil action," then no statutory provision authorizes federal-court subject-matter jurisdiction. The Supreme Court noted this problem of a lack of statutory authorization in *Finley v. United States*, and it urged Congress to fix it with implementing legislation.[50]

76. Congress answered *Finley*'s call in 1990 with the supplemental-jurisdiction statute.[51] The statute subsumed the prior judicial doctrines of pendent and ancillary jurisdiction into a new statutory authorization of supplemental jurisdiction. It also attempted to codify much of the Court's doctrine as set out in *Gibbs* and *Owen Equipment.*

77. The supplemental-jurisdiction statute has three major components. First, the statute expressly confers on the federal district courts as much supplemental jurisdiction as the Constitution permits. For any civil action within the district courts'

49. 437 U.S. 365 (1978).
50. 490 U.S. 545 (1989).
51. 28 U.S.C. §1367.

original jurisdiction, the statute provides statutory authorization over such other claims that are "so related" to the original jurisdiction claims that they form one constitutional "case" or "controversy."[52] This first component effectively codifies the *Gibbs* test. Second, the statute withdraws supplemental jurisdiction from claims that present a risk of circumvention of the rule of complete diversity, such as the claim at issue in *Owen Equipment*. Of course, if the basis for original subject-matter jurisdiction is federal-question jurisdiction, no withdrawal is necessary, and the statute confirms that by limiting the withdrawal only to certain claims in diversity cases.[53] Third, the statute confirms the discretionary nature of the authorization of supplemental jurisdiction by granting federal courts discretion to keep or decline supplemental jurisdiction that is granted and not withdrawn by the statute. The statutory factors are analogous to the *Gibbs* factors for exercising discretion.[54]

78. The supplemental-jurisdiction statute is far more intricate than the federal-question statute or the diversity-jurisdiction statute. Unsurprising, then, although the drafters carefully tried to track the Supreme Court's own doctrine and to anticipate how best to accommodate the underlying policy implications of supplemental jurisdiction, they did not fully anticipate all the complexities of civil litigation that might be implicated by the statute. One such complexity is that the statutory language could be read as ambiguous in the following scenario. Say a California plaintiff sues a New York defendant for USD 100,000 and also wishes to sue a second defendant. If the second defendant is from California, then complete diversity would be lacking, and the policies underlying supplemental jurisdiction's preservation of the complete-diversity rule would be undermined by the extension of supplemental jurisdiction to the nondiverse claim. So, in that scenario, supplemental jurisdiction should not extend to the nondiverse claim. But say the second defendant is instead from Texas, but the claim against that defendant is only for USD 25,000. Now, the claim satisfies diversity of citizenship but still would be ineligible for diversity jurisdiction because it fails the amount-in-controversy test. An argument nevertheless exists for extending supplemental jurisdiction to such a claim because the additional amount merely *adds* to the amount in controversy over the whole case, which already was met by the USD 100,000 claim against the New Yorker. The problem is that the supplemental-jurisdiction statute does not contain language expressly distinguishing between a defect in complete diversity and a defect in the amount in controversy. In 2005, the Supreme Court resolved the issue by holding, in a somewhat tortured reading of the statute, that a defect in complete diversity disqualifies all claims from both diversity jurisdiction and supplemental jurisdiction but that a defect in one claim's amount in controversy could be segregated as a separate claim eligible for supplemental jurisdiction.[55]

79. As mentioned above, the supplemental-jurisdiction statute is unique in expressly granting discretion to federal district courts over a small part of their own

52. *Ibid.*, §1367(a).
53. *Ibid.*, §1367(b).
54. *Ibid.*, §1367(c).
55. *Exxon Corp. v. Allapattah Servs. Inc.*, 545 U.S. 546 (2005).

subject-matter jurisdiction. That statutory authorization can be seen as congressional deference to the expertise of federal courts in being able to assess, in the context of a specific case, whether the exercise of federal-court jurisdiction over a nondiverse state-law claim best accommodates the competing policy tensions underlying supplemental jurisdiction. Such discretion always presents risks of abuse and inconsistent application, but the lack of widespread criticism of federal courts' exercise of discretion in this context suggests that federal courts are exercising discretion within acceptable bounds.

V. Removal

A. Principles

80. Because most federal subject-matter jurisdiction is concurrently granted to both the federal courts and the state courts, the plaintiff usually has the initial choice to file the lawsuit in either state or federal court. A plaintiff's choice to file in state court can, however, undermine the purposes of federal subject-matter jurisdiction. For example, a California plaintiff who files a diversity case against a New York defendant in California state court would undermine the purpose of diversity jurisdiction, which is to protect an out-of-state party from any home-state biases that a state court might harbor. Somewhat differently, a California plaintiff who files a federal-question case against a defendant in California state court deprives the federal courts of the opportunity to adjudicate federal claims while foisting the case upon California state courts, which might not wish to devote time and resources to it. To curtail a plaintiff's ability to select state court in circumstances detrimental to the defendant or to federal interests, Congress has long provided the defendant with an ability to "remove" such a case from state court to federal court.[56]

81. Removal is a one-way ratchet. It allows the defendant to transfer the case from state court to federal court. Removal does not allow a party to transfer a case from federal court to state court. Once a case is filed originally in federal court, it may not be transferred to a state court. However, a case that has been removed from state to federal court may, under circumstances discussed below, be remanded back from the federal court to the state court where it was initially filed. Remand also is a one-way ratchet that exists solely to "undo" an improper removal.

82. Only the defendant may remove a case. Plaintiffs may not remove. After all, plaintiffs get the initial choice of forum, and those that choose state court ought not get to change their minds later for a second chance at federal court.

---

56. 28 U.S.C. §1441.

83. Removal is of the whole case. A defendant cannot remove part of a case. If a case involves claims that are removable and claims that are nonremovable, the defendant can remove the whole case, subject to possible remand of the nonremovable parts.[57]

B. Basis for Removal

84. The removal statute does not generally alter the subject-matter jurisdiction of the federal courts. For most cases, only those that could have been filed in federal court originally are eligible to be removed to federal court.[58] For that reason, the same rules that would apply to subject-matter jurisdiction under federal-question jurisdiction, diversity jurisdiction, and alienage jurisdiction apply to removability.

85. Congress has, however, made some claims that could have been filed in federal court nonremovable. Claims under workmen's compensation statutes and the Federal Employers' Liability Act, for example, are specifically nonremovable.[59] These exemptions reflect a policy choice to prioritize the plaintiff's initial forum choice. Another key type of case that is nonremovable is a diversity case filed in a state court located in a defendant's home state.[60] The reason for that exemption is that the rationale of diversity jurisdiction—providing a neutral federal forum to alleviate the possibility of state bias in favor of an in-state citizen—should not apply to an in-state defendant.

C. Removal Procedure

86. The removal of an action is to the federal court in the same geographic region as the state court where the case was filed.[61] Removal is a transfer across judicial systems, not a transfer across geographic locations.

87. The general removal statute requires that all defendants join in or consent to removal.[62] This unanimity requirement forces multiple defendants to act as a single unit when electing federal court.

88. Removal occurs when a defendant files, in the applicable federal court, a notice of removal.[63] The notice must provide a short and plain statement of the basis for removal, along with all papers filed in the state court. The defendant must then

---

57. 28 U.S.C. §1441(c).
58. Exceptions include claims against federal officers under 28 U.S.C. §1442(a). *See Mesa v. California*, 489 U.S. 121, 136 (1989).
59. 28 U.S.C. §1445.
60. *Ibid.*, §1441(b).
61. *Ibid.*, §1441(a).
62. *Ibid.*, §1446(b)(2).
63. *Ibid.*, § 1446(a).

serve the notice on all parties and file the notice with the state court. Importantly, the notice is not a motion. No court approval is required for a defendant to remove the case. Once the notice is filed, the case is removed, even if removed improperly. (The propriety of removal is tested on a motion for remand, discussed below.)

89. The notice must be filed within thirty days after the defendant has received court papers indicating that the case is removable. Often, that time period will begin at the time the state-court complaint is initially served on the defendant.[64] However, sometimes, a case is not removable at the time of initial filing. For example, a California plaintiff may sue a California defendant and a New York defendant, each for USD 100,000, for state-law claims. Such a case is not removable because it lacks complete diversity. But if, six months later, the California defendant is dismissed from the lawsuit, leaving only a California plaintiff and a New York defendant, then the case suddenly meets the requirements for diversity jurisdiction and has become removable. At that time, the defendant has thirty days to file a notice of removal.[65]

90. Each defendant gets its own thirty days to remove the case. Thus, if a California plaintiff sues a New York defendant and a Texas defendant, and the plaintiff serves the New York defendant on January 1 and the Texas defendant on January 15, each defendant has thirty days from the day it is served to remove the case. The Texas defendant, therefore, can remove the case on February 2, even though that date is outside the thirty-day window for the New York defendant to file a removal notice. No deadline limits when defendants can consent to a removal notice filed by another defendant.

91. An additional timing barrier applies to diversity cases. Cases removable solely on grounds of diversity are removable only within one year after they are initially filed.[66] The rationale is that removal is very disruptive to a case that has been litigated in the original state court for a period of time. That disruption is accepted when removal is based on a federal question because of the importance of making federal courts available to hear and adjudicate federal issues. But that disruption outweighs the need for diversity jurisdiction. An exception to the one-year bar is if the plaintiff has, in bad faith, manipulated the removability of the case to take advantage of the one-year bar. If so, the one-year bar will not apply to bar removal.[67]

D. Remand

92. Once the case has been removed to federal court, the plaintiff or a nonconsenting defendant can move to remand the case back to state court based on some defect in removal. For defects in removal that pertain to removal procedure—such

64. *Murphy Brothers, Inc. v. Michetti Pipe Stringing, Inc.*, 526 U.S. 344 (1999).
65. 28 U.S.C. §1446(b)(3).
66. *Ibid.*, §1446(c)(1).
67. *Ibid.*, §1446(c)(1).

as a violation of the unanimity rule or noncompliance with the thirty-day deadline—the motion to remand must be filed within thirty days of removal.[68] Failure to timely move to remand is deemed a waiver of those defects in removal, and the case will remain in federal court despite those defects. However, if the defects are in the subject-matter jurisdiction of the federal court, such as if a state-law case is removed despite a lack of complete diversity, then the court must remand the case whenever the defect is discovered, and no remand motion is required. A federal court exercising supplemental jurisdiction may remand supplemental claims (but not federal-question or diversity claims) at any time under the discretion granted by the supplemental-jurisdiction statute.[69]

93. A district court's order remanding the case to state court is not appealable.[70] A district court's order refusing to remand, however, is appealable after final judgment.

§2. Personal Jurisdiction

I. Factors to be Taken into Account

94. The term "personal jurisdiction" within American law is a modern amalgam of the two types of judicial jurisdiction historically exercised by common-law courts: jurisdiction in personam is the power of a court over a party, and jurisdiction in rem is the power of a court over property.

95. Although the geographic allocation of cases among courts in the United States depends upon typical factors of litigation convenience, three other factors substantially complicate the inquiry. The first is the constitutional right of due process of law, which establishes an unalterable outer bound of how unrelated a forum can be to the litigation and parties and still enter a binding judgment. This factor is framed as an individual litigant right, which, like other rights, can be waived by the rightsholder. Following this principle, matters of territorial allocation under both personal jurisdiction and venue have long been waivable rights such that the inconvenienced party can submit to the power of the court. That personal jurisdiction and venue can be waived or consented to makes these case-allocation doctrines fundamentally different from subject-matter jurisdiction.[71]

96. The second factor is the federal structure of the United States. That federal structure has vertical (i.e., national-state) dimensions and horizontal (i.e., state-state) dimensions. The vertical dimensions mean that state-court systems are completely different judicial systems from the federal-court system, and states have no authority to allocate cases among federal courts, even among federal courts that sit

68. *Ibid.*, §1447(c).
69. *Carnegie-Mellon University v. Cohill*, 484 U.S. 343 (1988).
70. 28 U.S.C. §1447(d).
71. *Insurance Corp. of Ireland, Ltd. v. Compagnie des Bauxites de Guinee*, 456 U.S. 694 (1982).

within their territorial borders. The horizontal dimensions mean that each state has the authority to allocate cases geographically among courts within its borders but has no authority to allocate cases outside its borders; in addition, the allocation of cases among states implicates the harmonious relationship of the states within a single union.

97. The third factor is the large and culturally diverse territorial expanse of the United States. The burdens on a defendant from rural Maine to defend in a court on a remote Hawaiian island 5,000 miles and five time zones away may be significant. Further, the litigation culture, norms, and practices in California state courts may be quite different from those of Louisiana state court. Even the substantive law that applies to the parties' dispute can depend upon where the lawsuit is heard. (The states have not adopted any interstate compact establishing uniform choice-of-law or territorial-authority principles.) The location of the dispute, in other words, can matter a great deal.

II. Personal Jurisdiction in State Court

A. *Constitutional Limits*

1. Overview and Historical Development

98. For the first ninety years after the current government of the United States was formed by the ratification of the federal Constitution in 1788, individual states were free to fashion their own rules of territorial jurisdiction as they saw fit, subject only to the constraint that a state court's judgment exceeding jurisdictional norms might be denied recognition by other states or by the federal courts. The Full Faith and Credit Clause, along with implementing federal statute,[72] provided a basis for the Supreme Court to review one state's refusal to honor the judgment of another state, and, during this initial ninety-year period, the Supreme Court would occasionally do so. But the Supreme Court generally had no basis for reviewing a direct challenge to a state court's jurisdiction.

99. In 1878, however, the Court decided the famous *Pennoyer* case and held that the Due Process Clause of the Fourteenth Amendment, ratified in 1868, provided a basis for direct review of a state court's assertion of personal jurisdiction.[73] In *Pennoyer*, the Supreme Court held that a judgment entered without personal jurisdiction exceeded "due process of law."

100. Pennoyer also restated the traditional bases for establishing personal jurisdiction. A court had personal jurisdiction over a party who voluntarily appeared in court, who was a resident of the state, or who was served with a summons while physically within the territorial authority of the court, which, for state courts,

72. U.S. Const. Art. IV, §1; 28 U.S.C. §1738.
73. *Pennoyer v. Neff*, 95 U.S. (5 Otto) 714 (1877).

reached state borders. The Court reaffirmed that a state court always had *in rem* jurisdiction over property located within its borders. Personal jurisdiction at the time of *Pennoyer*, then, was set by state territorial boundaries.

101. This scheme of territorial jurisdiction had a decidedly "pro-defendant" tilt. Plaintiffs with claims against residents of other states generally faced the burden of filing suit in the home state of their adversaries. This became increasingly intolerable for two reasons. First, modern means of communication and transportation brought citizens of different states into virtually daily contact, often without either party to a transaction leaving their state of residence. Second, the business landscape changed to one in which the dominant form of commercial enterprise was the corporation, a legally fictitious "person" whose "presence" in a particular state at a particular time was a legal and metaphysical construct rather than an objective fact of physical reality.

102. States adapted to this new environment by conditioning the right to engage in activity in the state on consent to personal jurisdiction in the state. The theory behind these mechanisms made some sense from a fairness perspective: if a California citizen came into New York and, while there, caused harm in New York, New York courts should be able to adjudicate claims against that California citizen for those New York harms even if the citizen had returned to California and could no longer be served in New York. The mechanisms for extracting such consent varied. For businesses, states often conditioned the right to do business in the state on the business's consent to appointment of an in-state agent for purposes of in-state service of process.[74] For individuals, like car drivers or for other inherently dangerous activities, the state relied on implied consent articulated in the law.[75]

103. The attempts to fit modern cases into the rigid territorial pigeonholes of *Pennoyer* based on stretched—perhaps even fictitious—notions of presence and consent proved unsatisfying. In 1945, the Supreme Court adopted a new standard, based on fairness, for determining the constitutionality of state-court assertions of territorial jurisdiction.[76]

104. In *International Shoe*, the Supreme Court declared that personal jurisdiction over a nonconsenting nonresident served outside the state complied with constitutional due process when the defendant had "certain minimum contacts with it such that the maintenance of the suit does not offend "traditional notions of fair play and substantial justice."[77] The "minimum contacts" test is in addition to the traditional bases for satisfying due process of consent, residency, and in-state service.[78]

---

74. *Pennsylvania Fire Insurance Co. v. Gold Issue Mining & Milling Co.*, 243 U.S. 93 (1917).
75. *Hess v. Pawloski*, 274 U.S. 352 (1927).
76. *International Shoe Co. v. Washington*, 326 U.S. 310 (1945).
77. *Ibid.*, at 316. The Supreme Court has extended this "minimum contacts" test to in rem jurisdiction. *Shaffer v. Heitner*, 433 U.S. 186 (1977).
78. *Mallory v. Norfolk Southern Railway Co.*, 600 U.S. 122 (2023).

2. Constitutional Standards Detailed

a. Residency

105. Since *Pennoyer*, states have had personal jurisdiction over their residents, although the residency basis for personal jurisdiction often was conflated with the in-state service basis because a state's power to issue a summons stopped at its state borders, and service was necessary to compel appearance even of residents. Service rules were relaxed in the 1900s, and in *Milliken v. Meyer*, the Court confronted a case in Wyoming between Wyoming residents when the defendant was personally served in Colorado. The Court held that the locus of the residency was within Wyoming, and therefore, Wyoming had personal jurisdiction over the Wyoming resident for any cause of action, irrespective of where he happened to be at the time of service.[79]

b. In-State Service

106. Although older cases seemed to allow in-state-service-based personal jurisdiction over legal entities, the doctrine today is construed as being reserved for natural individuals. This method of obtaining personal jurisdiction—also called "tag jurisdiction" or "transient jurisdiction"—reflects the *Pennoyer*-era understanding that a state has personal jurisdiction over a person lawfully served with a summons while voluntarily and physically present in the state. It is at that very moment of service that personal jurisdiction, wholly within the territory of the state—becomes valid. The summons, too, is valid and compels appearance. Importantly, although the personal jurisdiction attaches only with respect to the particular lawsuit to which the summons pertains, the personal jurisdiction over the person served is for any claim within that lawsuit, wherever the claim arose and even if unrelated to the reasons why the person was in the state in the first place.

107. In 1990, in the case *Burnham v. Superior Court*, the Supreme Court upheld tag jurisdiction under circumstances stretching the limits of due process.[80] A husband and wife residing in New Jersey decided to divorce, and they planned to have New Jersey handle the divorce proceedings. But before any divorce action was initiated, the wife moved to California and initiated a divorce action in California, which had more favorable divorce laws for the wife than New Jersey had. While visiting California on a business matter (and to see his children), the husband was served with the California divorce summons. The Supreme Court unanimously upheld service and personal jurisdiction over the husband in California.

c. Consent

108. Because constitutional personal jurisdiction is sourced in the Due Process Clause and conceived of as an individual right, a court may assert jurisdiction over

79. 311 U.S. 457 (1940).
80. 495 U.S. 604 (1990).

a defendant otherwise beyond the court's territorial jurisdiction if the defendant consents to its jurisdiction, waives the constitutional right, or forfeits the procedural right to object.[81] Such a waiver may result from consent in advance of suit, from voluntary submission at the time of suit, or from other forms of conduct that give rise to a constructive waiver of the right to object.

109. Advance consent can be conferred by contract in which the parties subscribe to a forum-selection clause, thus agreeing in advance to submit to the territorial jurisdiction of the chosen forum. As with any other contractual provision, a forum selection clause may be disregarded as unconscionable under customary principles of contract law. But the Supreme Court has, under admiralty law, refused to invalidate forum-selection clauses just because they are contained in contracts of adhesion.[82]

110. Advanced consent can also be given by accepting a state's condition on the right to do business in the state. In *Mallory v. Norfolk Southern Railway Co.*, the Supreme Court held that a state could, consistent with the Due Process Clause, condition the right to do business in the state on a nonresident corporation's consent to personal jurisdiction in the state.[83] The Court upheld the state's exercise of personal jurisdiction over a registered corporation even though the cause of action arose elsewhere and had little connection to the forum state.

111. Voluntary submission at suit is manifested by the plaintiff invoking the jurisdiction of the court in the first instance[84] or by the defendant entering a "general appearance" in response to the service of process.[85] Most states provide a special procedure to allow the defendant to appear, especially for the purposes of challenging personal jurisdiction in the first responsive act; if the defendant's challenge is unsuccessful, the defendant's subsequent litigation of the case usually will not be deemed to be consent to personal jurisdiction.

112. If a defendant files to make a timely and proper special appearance challenging personal jurisdiction, the law deems the defendant to have waived the defense. This waiver rule applies in federal court as well.[86]

113. A defendant that properly preserves the issue of personal jurisdiction for decision by making a special appearance subjects itself to the power of the forum to adjudicate that issue. In the course of adjudicating that issue, the trial court may compel discovery on personal jurisdiction and may properly sanction a breach of its procedural rules by estopping the defendant from denying facts establishing personal jurisdiction.[87]

---

81. *Mallory v. Norfolk Southern Railway Co.*, 600 U.S. 122 (2023).
82. *Carnival Cruise Lines, Inc. v. Shute*, 499 U.S. 585 (1991).
83. 600 U.S. 122 (2023).
84. *Adam v. Saenger*, 303 U.S. 59 (1938).
85. *York v. Texas*, 137 U.S. 15 (1890).
86. Fed. R. Civ. P. 12(h).
87. *Insurance Corp. of Ireland, Ltd. v. Compagnie des Bauxites de Guinee*, 456 U.S. 694 (1982).

d. Minimum Contacts

114. The Supreme Court's cases developing *International Shoe*'s minimum-contacts test have recognized two distinct species of this form of personal jurisdiction: general jurisdiction (also called all-purpose personal jurisdiction) and specific jurisdiction (also called case-linked personal jurisdiction).

i General Jurisdiction

115. For many years, commentators and lower courts interpreted *International Shoe* and its progeny to validate the exercise of personal jurisdiction over a defendant that had "continuous and systematic" contacts with a state, even if the cause of action arose elsewhere and was unrelated to those contacts.[88] That test was commonly assumed to subject most national corporations to general jurisdiction in all fifty states. Notably, this form of all-purpose adjudicative jurisdiction was deemed exorbitant by most other countries.

116. In a set of two cases in the 2010s, the Court drastically scaled back the test for general jurisdiction. In *Goodyear Tires Dunlop Operations, S.A. v. Brown*, the Court held that general jurisdiction requires more than "continuous and systematic" contacts—it requires that the defendant's contacts with the state be so continuous and systematic as to render it "essentially at home" in the state, with paradigm examples being an individual's state of domicile or a corporation's state of incorporation and state of principal place of business.[89] In *Daimler AG v. Bauman*, the Court reaffirmed the "at home" test and its "paradigm examples" and further described the test as providing "at least one clear and certain forum" to sue the defendant for any and all claims and which would allow defendants to structure their primary conduct with general jurisdiction in mind.[90] The Court also rejected the test as a threshold determination and instead framed it as a comparative inquiry—where the defendant is *most* "at home."[91] The Court did leave open the possibility that, in an "exceptional case," a defendant might be "at home" in some place other than the paradigm locations, such as if a corporation temporarily relocated the center of its operations to a new state.[92]

ii Specific Jurisdiction

117. In contrast to general jurisdiction, which does not depend upon the claim, specific jurisdiction depends upon the "relationship among the defendant, the forum, and the litigation."[93] The test can be visualized as a triangle, with the defendant, the forum, and the claim each on a different point of the triangle and the sides

88. *See Helicopteros Nacionales de Colombia, S.A. v. Hall*, 466 U.S. 408, 417 (1984); *Perkins v. Benguet Consolidated Mining Co.*, 342 U.S. 437, 445–446 (1952).
89. 564 U.S. 915, 919, 924 (2011).
90. 571 U.S. 117, 137 (2014).
91. *Ibid.*, at 139 n. 20.
92. *Ibid.*, at 139 n. 19.
93. *Shaffer v. Heitner*, 433 U.S. 186, 204 (1977).

linking, each representing a requisite level of connectedness between the points. All sides of the triangle must be met for specific jurisdiction to be exercised.

118. The side of the triangle linking the claim to the forum was elaborated in *Bristol-Myers Squibb Co. v. Superior Court.*[94] There, consumers of the drug Plavix sued its manufacturer, BMS, in California state court. BMS is a Delaware company with its principal place of business in New York; it developed the drug in New York but distributed the drug throughout the United States. The plaintiffs included more than 600 consumers from around the country, including not only consumers from California who received, ingested, and were harmed by Plavix in California but also customers from other states, like Texas, who did none of those things in California. The Supreme Court held that the California court could not exercise specific jurisdiction over BMS with respect to the non-California plaintiffs because their particular claims had no connection to the California forum. Further, the Court held that the mere similarity of the non-California claims to California claims was irrelevant because specific jurisdiction is a claim-by-claim analysis that requires each claim to have a sufficient connection to the forum.

119. The side of the triangle linking the defendant to the forum has been the topic of most specific jurisdiction cases. The Supreme Court has admonished that the defendant must have "purposefully avail[ed] itself of the privilege of conducting activities within the forum State," thereby enjoying the "benefits and protection" of forum law.[95] In *International Shoe*, this factor was met by the defendant's use of in-state salesmen to solicit shoe orders that then resulted in the defendant shipping shoes into the state directly. In *World-Wide Volkswagen Corp. v. Woodson*, however, a local car dealership serving primarily customers in New York, Connecticut, and New Jersey was not subject to personal jurisdiction in Oklahoma when a car it sold was driven to, exploded in, and caused injury there because the dealership had not purposefully availed itself or targeted Oklahoma. And in *Walden v. Fiore*, the Court held that Nevada could not exercise specific jurisdiction over a state officer alleged to have unlawfully seized cash in Georgia even though the officer reasonably would have known that the plaintiffs would be harmed in Nevada by not having access to the cash there.[96] In each case, the question was whether the defendant's purposeful connection to the forum was sufficient.

120. Two significant issues regarding the sufficiency of connection between the defendant and the forum remain open. The first is the application of minimum contacts and purposefulness to virtual contacts, such as through the Internet. Whether a Delaware company that maintains a website accessible to consumers in Texas has established sufficient purposeful connection with Texas remains an important and widely litigated open question. The second is the sufficiency of the connection when the defendant uses a commercial intermediary, such as an independent distributor, to take advantage of the forum. The Court has been unable to muster a majority

94. 582 U.S. 255 (2017).
95. *World-Wide Volkswagen Corp. v. Woodson*, 444 U.S. 286, 297 (1980).
96. 571 U.S. 277 (2014).

opinion to provide guidance on such so-called "stream of commerce" cases. In *Asahi Metal Industry Co. v. Superior Court*, some justices would have found a sufficient connection when the defendant was reasonably aware that its products could cause injury in the state, while other justices would have found a connection only when the defendant took some affirmative action targeting that state, such as advertising in the state or customizing the product for specific distribution in that state. Neither view commanded a majority of the justices.[97] Similarly, in *J. McIntyre Machinery, Ltd. v. Nicastro*, a case ostensibly taken to resolve the *Asahi* split, the Court again failed to muster a majority opinion; it resolved the case on the extraordinarily narrow ground that mere awareness by the manufacturer that a product is likely to end up in a state through independent distribution channels is not enough when only *one* product actually does so.[98]

121. The third side of the triangle requires a connection between the defendant's forum-based conduct and the claim. In *Ford Motor Co. v. Montana Eighth Judicial District Court*, the Court held that the claim must arise out of or relate to that forum-based conduct.[99] In that case, two Ford cars caused in jury in Montana and Minnesota, respectively, and the plaintiffs sued Ford in those states of injury. No one disputed that the claims were related to forums—the injuries happened in those states. Nor did anyone dispute that Ford had substantial purposeful connections with those states by selling cars there and advertising there. Instead, Ford argued that its forum-based conduct was not sufficiently related to the claim because the particular cars that caused the injury were sold to customers in different states; the customers unilaterally took them, without Ford's knowledge, to the forum states. The Court rejected Ford's argument and found that Ford's conduct in those states was sufficiently related to the claim because its conduct in those states was geared toward encouraging drivers to drive their Ford cars—including the same makes and models as the specific cars at issue—in those specific states; thus, Ford's in-state conduct was related to the fact that those cars caused injury in those states.

122. In addition to requiring a tripartite test of affiliations, specific jurisdiction also requires that the assertion of personal jurisdiction comport with "traditional notions of fair play and substantial justice."[100] How this fairness component relates to the contacts analyses is unclear today. In *Burger King Corp. v. Rudzewicz*, the Court articulated five "fairness factors" that could raise or lower the minimum-contacts threshold: the burden on the defendant, the interest in the plaintiff in effective and efficient relief, the interest of the state in adjudicating the dispute, the interstate judicial system's interest in efficient resolution of controversies, and the shared interests of the states in furthering substantive social policies.[101] In *Asahi*, decided in 1987, those fairness factors were dispositive. But since *Asahi*, the Court has neither recited them nor applied them as a separate inquiry. Especially in light

97. 480 U.S. 102 (1987).
98. 564 U.S. 873 (2011).
99. 592 U.S. 351 (2021).
100. *International Shoe Co. v. Washington*, 326 U.S. 310, 316 (1945).
101. 471 U.S. 462, 477 (1985).

of some justices' discomfort with "[f]reeform notions of fundamental fairness" as a touchstone for specific jurisdiction[102] and other justices' seeming willingness to revisit past precedent,[103] it is unclear today what independent role, if any, the fairness factors play in the doctrine of specific jurisdiction.

B. State "Long-Arm" Statutes

123. The constitutional principles set an outer limit of a state court's exercise of personal jurisdiction. States can constrain their courts to exercise *less* personal jurisdiction than what the Constitution otherwise would allow. State laws that purport to set the scope of personal jurisdiction are called "long-arm statutes," which refers to the metaphorical image of the process of a state court reaching out (like a long arm) to grab defendants from other states. But the term is a double misnomer because state law can only limit, not expand, the scope of personal jurisdiction set by the Constitution, so the operative effect of many long-arm statutes is to restrain the exercise of state-court personal jurisdiction. And many state laws setting the scope of state-court jurisdiction are not statutes but rather are state constitutional provisions, rules of court, or even common-law doctrines developed by state courts themselves. Nevertheless, the moniker has stuck.

124. Some long-arm statutes authorize the full scope of territorial jurisdiction permitted by the federal Constitution. California's long-arm statute exemplifies this approach by providing: "A court of this state may exercise jurisdiction on any basis not inconsistent with the constitution of this state or of the United States."[104] In California and other like states, the sole inquiry for whether a state court has personal jurisdiction is the scope set by the Fourteenth Amendment.

125. Other long-arm statutes, however, are more detailed. For instance, New York's long-arm statute provides in pertinent part:

> Personal jurisdiction by acts of non-domiciliaries.
>
> (a) Acts which are the basis for jurisdiction. As to a cause of action arising from any of the acts enumerated in this section, a court may exercise personal jurisdiction over any non-domiciliary, or his executor of administrator, who in person or through an agent:
> (1) transacts any business within the state or contracts anywhere to supply goods and services in the state; or
> (2) commits a tortious act within the state, except as to a cause of action for defamation of character arising from the act; or

102. *Nicastro*, 564 U.S. at 880 (Kennedy, J., plurality).
103. *Ford*, 592 U.S. at 383 (Gorsuch, J., concurring).
104. Cal. Civ. Proc. Code §410.10.

(3) commits a tortious act without the state causing injury to person or property within the state, except as to a cause of action for defamation of character arising from the act, if he
   (i) regularly does or solicits business, or engages in any other persistent course of conduct, or derives substantial revenue from goods used or consumed or services rendered in the state, or
   (ii) expects or should reasonably expect the act to have consequences in the state and derives substantial revenue from interstate or international commerce; or
(4) owns, uses or possesses any real property situated within the state.[105]

126. When a state's long-arm statute takes this "laundry list" approach, seeking to enumerate specific factors that are determinative of territorial jurisdiction in a particular case, the possibility exists that territorial jurisdiction may be unavailable in that state with regard to a particular defendant in a particular case simply because the case and the defendant's conduct do not fall within one of the jurisdictional categories specified in the statute, even though the exercise of personal jurisdiction would otherwise be authorized by the U.S. Constitution. New York's highest court, the New York Court of Appeals, has construed the New York long-arm statute to indeed provide less jurisdictional authorization than the Constitution.[106] But other state courts of last resort have construed the facially restrictive language of similarly detailed long-arm statutes as nonetheless conferring the full scope of jurisdictional power permitted by the Constitution.[107]

III. Personal Jurisdiction in Federal Court

A. Constitutional Scope

127. The Fourteenth Amendment's Due Process Clause applies only to the states. The Fifth Amendment's Due Process Clause applies to the United States. Accordingly, the constitutional scope of federal courts' personal jurisdiction is set by the Fifth Amendment, which is not restricted to state borders. In 2025, the U.S. Supreme Court decided *Fuld v. Palestine Liberation Organization*,[108] holding that the test for state-court personal jurisdiction under the Fourteenth Amendment does not necessarily apply by analogy to the test for federal-court personal jurisdiction under the Fifth Amendment. The Court explained that the Fourteenth Amendment's restricts are designed, in part, to guard interstate federalism, while the Fifth Amendment is not. Accordingly, the Court reversed a lower federal court that had applied the "minimum contacts" test as a limit imposed by the Fifth Amendment. However, the Court did not decide what precise limits, if any, the Fifth Amendment imposes.

105. N.Y. C.P.L.R. §302(a).
106. *State v. Vayu, Inc.*, 39 N.Y.3d 330 (2023). *See also, e.g., Fraser v. Smith*, 594 F.3d 842, 848 (11th Cir. 2010) (Fla.); *Thomason v. Chem. Bank*, 661 A.2d 595, 602 (Conn. 1995).
107. E.g., *Pinner v. Pinner*, 225 A.3d 433, 443 (Md. 2020).
108. 606 U.S. _ (2025).

It seems likely that, at a minimum, all federal courts would have constitutional personal jurisdiction over all U.S. residents, all foreign parties served with process within the United States, all foreign parties with some level of connection to the United States as a whole, and all foreign parties who have consented to federal-court personal jurisdiction.

B. Statutory Restrictions

128. Although the Constitution sets very minimal restrictions on federal-court personal jurisdiction, Congress may limit federal courts' personal jurisdiction as it sees fit. In unusual contexts, Congress has authorized nationwide personal jurisdiction to the limits of the Fifth Amendment,[109] but, for the most part, the common understanding is that federal courts' exercise of personal jurisdiction is limited by Rule 4(k) of the Federal Rules of Civil Procedure, which states that serving a federal-court summons is effective to establish personal jurisdiction in federal court when the defendant would be subject to personal jurisdiction in a state court in the state in which the federal court sits.[110] In other words, Rule 4 has the effect of limiting a federal court's exercise of personal jurisdiction, in most cases, to the same scope that a state court would have. Thus, for questions of personal jurisdiction governed by Rule 4(k)(1)(A), personal jurisdiction in federal court indirectly depends upon the Fourteenth Amendment's limits and any long-arm statute's restrictions imposed on the state where the federal court is located.

129. Rule 4 itself provides for two other quite limited exceptions to the normally state-by-state scope of federal territorial jurisdiction. First, a federal district court may reach beyond state lines—but only within a radius of 100 miles from where the court sits—to assert territorial jurisdiction over additional defendants whose joinder is required for just adjudication of the main litigation.[111] Second, a federal district court may exercise nationwide jurisdiction in any federal-question case in which a particular defendant is not subject to the territorial jurisdiction of any state.[112]

109. E.g., 15 U.S.C. §25 (antitrust cases).
110. Fed. R. Civ. P. 4(k)(1)(A).
111. Fed. R. Civ. P. 4(k)(1)(B).
112. Fed. R. Civ. P. 4(k)(2).

Chapter 2. Venue and Forum Non Conveniens

§1. Venue in Federal Court

130. Venue refers to the allocation of cases within a judicial system for reasons of convenience and efficiency. In federal court, venue is neither constitutional nor jurisdictional.

131. Congress has provided for some specialized venue rules, but the general venue statute governs most civil actions.[113] Under that statute, venue is proper in any federal district: (1) in which any defendant resides if all defendants reside in the same state or (2) in which a substantial part of the events or omissions giving rise to the claim occurred, or a substantial part of property that is the subject of the action is situated. If no venue is proper under these provisions, the statute makes venue proper in any federal district in which any defendant is subject to the court's personal jurisdiction. For purposes of proper venue, defendant not resident in the United States can be sued in any federal district.

132. The defense of improper venue is a waivable defense that must be made, if at all, in the first response by a defendant.[114] A federal court without proper venue may, on proper motion, dismiss the case or transfer it, in the interests of justice, to a district court with jurisdiction and proper venue.[115] For cases calling for the application of state law on the substance of a claim, the transferee court will apply the choice-of-law rules of its host state, not of the transferor court's host state.

133. Even when jurisdiction and venue are both proper, the case may be filed in a district that is not the most convenient for the parties and witnesses. Accordingly, the venue-transfer statute allows for a federal district court with jurisdiction and venue to transfer the case to another district court with jurisdiction and venue (or to which all parties have consented) for the convenience of the parties and witnesses and in the interests of justice.[116] The usual rule for transfers from a proper venue to another proper venue (or venue by consent) is that the transferee court will, for state-law claims, apply the choice-of-law rules of the transferor's state.[117]

134. Parties can contractually consent to venue in advance of litigation through forum-selection clauses. When the parties select a venue that is not the venue chosen for filing the litigation by the plaintiff, the parties' contract does not make the venue where the case is filed improperly. Instead, the court should transfer the case to the district court selected by the parties' contract unless extraordinary reasons

113. 28 U.S.C. §1391.
114. Fed. R. Civ. P. 4(h).
115. 28 U.S.C. §1406(a).
116. *Ibid.*, § 1404(a).
117. *Ferens v. John Deere Co.*, 494 U.S. 516 (1990).

unrelated to the convenience of the parties militate keeping the case. When transfer is based on a forum-selection clause, the transferee court will apply its own state's choice-of-law rules to any state claim.[118]

135. Congress provided for a special kind of venue transfer for mass torts and other types of lawsuits that broadly fall under the term "multidistrict litigation" (MDL). This form of venue transfer is coupled with consolidation of many individual actions before a single judge for pretrial proceedings.[119] The idea is to harness the benefits and efficiencies of aggregation. Say, for example, a chemical herbicide is found to have carcinogenic properties. Each individual harmed can sue the same defendant individually around the country, but thousands of individual lawsuits all litigating common issues waste party and court resources. Class actions, with their stringent requirements, might not be available to aggregate such claims, as discussed in more detail below. But MDL transfer enables consolidation of all those individual lawsuits for aggregated treatment. MDL transfer is allowed when lawsuits sharing a common issue of law or fact should, for the convenience of the parties and witnesses and in the interests of justice and efficiency, be heard together. Unlike the general venue-transfer statute, MDL transfer is ordered by a special Judicial Panel on MDL comprised of sitting federal judges appointed to the Panel by the Chief Justices of the U.S. Supreme Court. Transfer is for pretrial matters only—trials can occur only in the transferor courts[120]—but the MDL court can enter all other orders, including dismissal orders, summary judgment, and approval of global settlement. MDL transfers have been heavily used in the last three decades, resolving perhaps more than a million individual cases in an aggregated fashion. In 2023, an MDL settlement of USD 6 billion resolved nearly 250,000 individual consolidated cases, all claiming injuries caused by a hearing-protection device.

§2. Forum Non Conveniens in Federal Court

136. This doctrine permits a court voluntarily to relinquish the territorial jurisdiction that it might otherwise exercise based on the availability of a more appropriate forum. In *Gulf Oil Corp. v. Gilbert*, the Supreme Court confirmed the inherent power of a federal court to dismiss pursuant to *forum non conveniens* even though the court has both jurisdiction and proper venue.[121] The Court directed consideration of both private and public factors, including the conveniences of the parties and the efficiency needs of the litigation, administrative congestion of the court, the interests of another community in adjudicating its own local disputes, and the like.[122] In *Piper Aircraft Co. v. Reyno*, the Supreme Court again upheld the discretionary power of a federal court to dismiss under the doctrine of *forum non conveniens* even when the substantive law to be applied in the alternate forum would

118. *Atlantic Marine Construction Co. v. United States District Court*, 571 U.S. 49 (2013).
119. 28 U.S.C. § 1407(a).
120. *Lexecon Inc. v. Milberg Weiss Bershad Hynes & Lerach*, 523 U.S. 26 (1998). A different rule for certain antitrust cases is provided by 28 U.S.C. §1407(g).
121. 330 U.S. 501 (1947).
122. *Ibid.*, at 508–509.

be less favorable to the plaintiff; the degree of unfavorability is merely one factor in the calculus.[123] The doctrine gives a strong presumption in favor of the plaintiff's chosen if the chosen forum is the plaintiff's home jurisdiction but not if the plaintiff has chosen some other forum.[124]

137. In federal court, the doctrine of *forum non conveniens* is governed by federal law, even if state or foreign law applies to the substantive claim to be adjudicated. The domestic application of the doctrine has been superseded by the federal interdistrict transfer statute, 28 U.S.C. §1404, discussed above. The doctrine is more relevant in federal court when a foreign court is available and more appropriate to resolve the dispute.

§3. State Courts

138. Each state uses state venue law, which varies from state to state, to allocate cases among its courts. As in federal court, most state courts have discretion to transfer any lawsuit to any other state court within the state in which the lawsuit might be more conveniently or efficiently adjudicated. No state has formal power to transfer a case to state courts in another state or to a federal court wherever located. The sole state-law mechanism for reallocating a case from one state's court to a court outside that state's judicial system is through the forum state's own version of *forum non conveniens*, which most states have adopted using rules similar to those followed in the federal courts.

§4. Resolution of Jurisdictional Conflicts

139. No special court within the American system resolves jurisdictional conflicts. The highest court of each system—the high court of each state system and the U.S. Supreme Court of the federal system—resolves challenges to jurisdiction and venue, just as it does for any other unsettled question of that system's law.

140. The default judgment of a court that lacked jurisdiction can be challenged as invalid in another court in the same or different judicial system. Indeed, the famous case *Pennoyer v. Neff* was just such a dispute, in which an Oregon state court entered a default judgment against defendant Neff, who had not appeared. In a subsequent proceeding in Oregon federal court, Neff challenged the validity of the state-court judgment on the ground that the state court had lacked personal jurisdiction over him in that proceeding. The Supreme Court agreed with Neff and held the Oregon state-court judgment to be invalid. This so-called collateral attack—challenging the validity of a judgment in a different proceeding—can only be used to challenge the default judgment on jurisdictional grounds.[125]

123. 454 U.S. 235 (1981).
124. *Ibid.*, at 255–256.
125. *Baldwin v. Iowa State Traveling Men's Ass'n*, 283 U.S. 522 (1931).

Chapter 3. International Jurisdiction

§1. Rules Applicable in the Absence of a Treaty

141. The previous discussion of the domestic jurisdiction of state and federal courts is fully applicable to the assertion of U.S. judicial jurisdiction over foreign parties or foreign disputes. The international context of litigation and the special burdens imposed on foreign litigants when summoned before U.S. courts are factors influencing the reasonableness of an assertion of judicial jurisdiction over a foreign defendant. And the doctrine of forum non conveniens, discussed above, is most justified when transnational parties or issues are involved. But, with few exceptions, state and federal laws do not formally give special treatment to foreign parties or transnational issues.

142. The key exceptions tend to *authorize*, rather than exclude, judicial jurisdiction in matters involving foreign defendants or transnational issues. As previously discussed, the Constitution and the diversity-jurisdiction statute specifically give federal courts subject-matter jurisdiction over suits involving foreign nationals. Rule 4(k)(2) of the Federal Rules of Civil Procedure specifically authorizes federal-court personal jurisdiction over foreign defendants when not otherwise prohibited by federal law.[126] And the Foreign Sovereign Immunities Act grants federal district courts jurisdiction over foreign states, officials, and state-owned corporations.[127]

143. One special federal statute authorizes federal district courts to order discovery of a party found within the court's district for use in proceedings before a foreign tribunal.[128] The nationality of the party is irrelevant; the party need only be found within the district and possess discoverable information relevant to a foreign proceeding. The Federal Rules applicable to ordinary discovery also govern the discovery proceedings ordered under this statute.

§2. International Treaties

144. The United States is a signatory to the 1964 Hague Service Convention, which is binding on both state and federal courts.[129] The Hague Convention governs the manner in which the process of American courts may be served abroad on defendants within other signatory countries. It provides a small measure of additional protection for foreign litigants against whom default judgments have been entered by American courts without compliance with the Hague Convention's directives. But, like all challenges to default judgments based on improper service, the challenge is restricted to jurisdictional and service-related defects; the defendant

126. Fed. R. Civ. P. 4(k)(2).
127. U.S.C. §§1330(b), 1608.
128. 28 U.S.C. §1782.
129. *Volkswagenwerk Aktiengesellschaft v. Schlunk*, 486 U.S. 694 (1988).

concedes the merits of the case. As a matter of risk avoidance, then, foreign defendants often prefer to appear in the U.S. court for purposes of filing a motion to dismiss for insufficient service of process or, in the alternative, for forum non conveniens.

Part III. The Civil Litigation Process

Chapter 1. Pleadings and Service

§1. Complaint

145. The complaint is a written document that sets out the legal claims for relief. (A "claim" is synonymous with a "cause of action," a term used by many state systems.) Filing the complaint commences the civil action.[130]

146. The Federal Rules of Civil Procedure, which govern pleading in federal court, have drastically simplified pleading from the technical process that it had been prior to 1938. The rules generally allow only complaints (for asserting claims) and answers (for responding to claims).[131] The form of the complaint is transsubstantive, in that, with limited exceptions, the standards for proper pleading of a claim in the complaint do not depend upon the particular claim. Those standards are designed to be extremely liberal; the rulemakers intended for even a layperson to be able to successfully plead a claim. In general, the primary goal of the complaint is simply to provide the defendant with notice of the claim and the grounds on which it rests.[132]

147. Implementing that intent, Rule 8 requires that the complaint contain only three things: a "short and plain statement of the grounds for the court's jurisdiction," a "short and plain statement of the claim showing that the pleader is entitled to relief," and a "demand for the relief sought." The first and third requirements can be established in a sentence. Depending upon the circumstances, so can the second. Indeed, the following sentences alone likely suffice to successfully plead a claim in a complaint: "On May 1, 2024, at the corner of McAllister St. and Hyde St. in San Francisco, the defendant, a resident of this state, negligently drove his car through a red light and struck plaintiff, a resident of a different state, while the plaintiff was crossing the street, causing the plaintiff injuries to his person. Plaintiff seeks $100,000 in damages. This court has diversity jurisdiction and personal jurisdiction." Of course, not all claims are so simple to plead, as explained in more detail below. But some are.

---

130. Fed. R. Civ. P. 3.
131. Fed. R. Civ. P. 7(a).
132. *Conley v. Gibson*, 355 U.S. 41 (1957).

148. The complaint is composed of *allegations*, which are statements that the party intends to prove at trial. The complaint is not verified, nor need it be accompanied by a sworn declaration, nor need the plaintiff attach any evidence. The rules direct that the exchange of factual information and the presentation of evidence occur after each party has pleaded its allegations. Unless Congress has directed otherwise, no judicial official screens the complaint as a matter of course. Instead, the court generally relies on the defendant to bring any deficiencies in the complaint to the court's attention.

149. Rule 8 confirms the liberal standard for pleading claims. It states that "[e]ach allegation must be simple, concise, and direct."[133] It also allows for pleading inconsistent statements or in the alternative.[134] For example, if a plaintiff in a car accident knows that either Bob or Ann was driving the car but is not sure which one was, the plaintiff can sue both Bob and Ann in the same lawsuit and allege both that Bob was driving and that Ann was driving. The allegations cannot both be true, but the federal pleading rules do not mind. The idea of pleading is to put allegations into contention. Which allegations have evidentiary truth will be determined by the defendants' answers, discovery, or, ultimately, trial.

150. Rule 8's liberal pleading standard does not mean that a plaintiff can make allegations without some reasonable foundation or knowingly make false statements. As discussed below, Rule 11 requires the plaintiff to have some good-faith basis for making each allegation. But the plaintiff need not provide that good-faith basis at the time of the pleading. The point of pleadings is simply to identify what issues will be litigated in the case. Resolution of those issues on the facts will be determined later.

151. Although the liberal standard of Rule 8 applies to most types of claims, a different standard applies to fraud claims. Rule 9 provides that "a party must state with particularity the circumstances constituting fraud."[135] The rulemakers believed that fraud was easy to allege, difficult to dispute, and inherently damaging to personal and business reputations, and therefore that plaintiffs should be required to identify the fraudulent circumstances with more specificity—the who, what, when, where. The Rule 9 standard remains based solely on allegations and is fairly easy to plead—it requires slightly more detail about the circumstances.

152. Even when a claim can be pleaded simply, easily, and concisely, common attorney practice is to add far more detail than necessary in complaints. Complaints commonly exceed thirty pages. One reason is that the complaint is a public opportunity to tell the plaintiff's story—and perhaps to show the defendant that the plaintiff means business.

---

133. Fed. R. Civ. P. 8(d).
134. Fed. R. Civ. P. 8(d).
135. Fed. R. Civ. P. 9(b).

§2. SERVICE OF PROCESS

153. Once the complaint has been drafted, it is signed by the attorney and filed with the court. The clerk of the court then gives the plaintiff a summons, which is a court order directing the defendant to answer the complaint.

154. The summons and a copy of the complaint (together, called "process") must be served on the defendant to give the defendant notice of the complaint and establish the court's authority to issue a default against the defendant if the defendant fails to appear. Normally, the defendant must be served within ninety days after the filing of the complaint, though the judge can extend that time for good cause.[136]

155. Anyone over the age of 18 and not a party may serve the defendant.[137] Typically, plaintiffs employ specialized process servers to do so. Process servers can be highly adept at locating and serving defendants who are trying to avoid service.

156. The Federal Rules provide detailed instructions for properly serving different categories of defendant. An individual defendant located in the United States may be served as allowed by state law of the state in which the district court sits, through personal service, by delivering process at the defendant's residence or usual place of abode to someone of suitable age and discretion who resides there, or by serving the defendant's appointed agent.[138] Celebrities often appoint an agent to avoid the disruption and public embarrassment of personal service. A business entity in the United States may be served as allowed by state law, upon an agent appointed to receive process, or by delivering process to an officer or managing agent.[139]

157. An individual in a foreign country may be served by any internationally agreed means reasonably calculated to give notice, or, if that option is not available, by any means reasonably calculated to give notice allowed by the country where the defendant is served, by personal service, by using mail that requires a signed receipt, or as ordered by the court.[140] A business entity may be served in a foreign country by any of these means other than personal service.[141]

158. In lieu of formal service, the plaintiff can ask the defendant to waive service by sending the defendant a copy of the summons and complaint through some common means, such as email, along with two copies of a waiver form prescribed by the Federal Rules. If the defendant completes and returns the waiver form, the defendant is deemed to have been effectively served. As a reward for not avoiding service, the Federal Rules give the defendant extra time—sixty days instead of the usual twenty-one—to respond to the complaint. If the defendant refuses to waive

136. Fed. R. Civ. P. 4(m).
137. Fed. R. Civ. P. 4(c)(2).
138. Fed. R. Civ. P. 4(e).
139. Fed. R. Civ. P. 4(h)(1).
140. Fed. R. Civ. P. 4(f).
141. Fed. R. Civ. P. 4(h)(2).

service without good cause, then the plaintiff must formally serve the defendant through the specified means under Rule 4, but the defendant will be liable for the plaintiff's costs of service.[142]

159. Underlying the service rules is the value of notice, a fundamental litigation right memorialized in the Magna Carta and now encompassed within the Due Process Clauses of the U.S. Constitution. Importantly, actual notice is not required; rather, the method used to serve the defendant must be reasonably calculated to give actual notice.[143] Normally, all the methods of service prescribed in Rule 4 are reasonably calculated to give actual notice, but the rule incorporates state methods, and some states might use methods that approach the bounds of the notice requirement.

160. For example, in *Jones v. Flowers*,[144] the Supreme Court applied the due-process notice principles to hold that when a state sent a certified letter to a homeowner at the home address to notify him of an impending tax sale caused by delinquent property taxes, and the state was made aware that the letter went "unclaimed," the state was then under an obligation to pursue other reasonable means of notice prior to instituting the tax sale. Such other means might include sending a regular first-class letter to the home, which letter (unlike the certified letter) might stay there long enough to be picked up by the property owner, or posting a notice of tax sale on the property itself.

§3. The Defendant's Response

161. Once the defendant has been served or has waived service, the defendant has three options. The first option is that the defendant can refuse to appear and suffer a default judgment. The defendant can then challenge the validity of the default judgment in a different proceeding. This challenge is called a *collateral attack*. It allows a different court to invalidate the default judgment. The justification for invalidation on collateral attack is very limited—generally, only a lack of jurisdiction or insufficient notice will suffice. The defendant is not allowed to challenge the default judgment on any other grounds, such as any nonjurisdictional defenses or factual contentions on the merits. The advantage of this approach is that the defendant can challenge the jurisdiction of the first court in a different court that may be more favorable or convenient to the defendant. A collateral attack generally is only available to challenge a default judgment; thus, if the defendant uses either of the other two options, any resulting judgment generally cannot be collaterally attacked in a different court (though it can be challenged on direct appeal).

162. The second option is that the defendant can file a preanswer motion. The third option is that the defendant can file an answer. Both options are described in more detail below.

142. Fed. R. Civ. P. 4(d).
143. *Mullane v. Hanover Bank & Trust*, 339 U.S. 309 (1950).
144. 547 U.S. 220 (2006).

I. Preanswer Motion to Dismiss

163. Rule 12 authorizes the defendant to file a preanswer motion to dismiss the complaint prior to answering with their own pleading. The motion, if it is filed, must be filed within twenty-one days after service (or sixty days after waiving service).[145]

164. A preanswer motion to dismiss can be based on any of seven defenses:

1. lack of subject-matter jurisdiction;
2. lack of personal jurisdiction;
3. improper venue;
4. insufficient process, referring to some defect in the contents of the process served on the defending party;
5. insufficient service of process, referring to some defect in the manner in which process was served on the defending party rather than the contents of what was received by the defending party;
6. failure to state a claim upon which relief can be granted, referring to the legal insufficiency of the claim even if the facts alleged in support of the claim are assumed to be true; and
7. failure to join a party under Rule 19, the Federal Rule of Civil Procedure governing joinder of parties deemed necessary to the just adjudication of a civil action.[146]

165. Of these defenses, motions to dismiss based on Rule 12(b)(6) are the most common. The test for deciding when a complaint "fail[s] to state a claim upon which relief can be granted" has shifted over the last few decades. In *Conley v. Gibson*, the Supreme Court stated that such a motion should be granted only if, accepting the allegations in the complaint as true, "it appears beyond doubt that the plaintiff can prove no set of facts in support of his claim which would entitle him to relief."[147] *Conley* set a standard of *legal sufficiency* that largely did not permit inquiry into the factual sufficiency of the complaint. In other words, a complaint could be dismissed if it pleaded a claim that the law did not recognize but not if it pleaded a recognized claim uncontroverted by the pleaded factual allegations. Lower federal courts resisted this liberal pleading regime, at times requiring specific factual allegations or requiring some showing of factual sufficiency to survive a motion to dismiss, but the Supreme Court twice rejected those heightened pleading standards and reaffirmed *Conley*.[148]

145. Fed. R. Civ. P. 12(a).
146. Fed. R. Civ. P. 12(b).
147. 355 U.S. 41, 46 (1957).
148. *Swierkiewicz v. Sorema N.A.*, 534 U.S. 506 (2002); *Leatherman v. Tarrant County Narcotics Intelligence & Coordination Unit*, 507 U.S. 163 (1993).

166. In 2006, however, the Supreme Court decided *Bell Atlantic Corp. v. Twombly.*[149] There, a class of telecommunications consumers sued several telecommunications providers for civil conspiracy under antitrust law. Antitrust law recognized such a civil claim but required, as a matter of proof, the plaintiff to show that the defendants entered into an agreement to restrain trade. The plaintiffs lacked such direct proof but nevertheless alleged an agreement and supported that allegation with other allegations of conscious parallel conduct—allegations that the defendants engaged in and knew of each other's anticompetitive conduct. Because such conduct *could* be the result of an antitrust conspiracy, the plaintiffs' allegations met the *Conley* standard because additional facts could show the existence or inference of an agreement to restrain trade. Nevertheless, the Supreme Court ordered the case dismissed under Rule 12(b)(6). The Court "retire[d]" the "no set of facts" standard from *Conley* and established a new factual-sufficiency standard that required the complaint to state a claim that was "plausible" under the facts alleged.[150] Further, the Court held that the plaintiffs' allegation of an agreement was not entitled to a presumption of truth because it was, according to the Court, merely a legal conclusion to be inferred from the allegations of conscious parallel conduct, not an additional allegation of fact. Having disregarded the direct allegation of an agreement, the Court then assessed the plausibility of an antitrust conspiracy as the cause of the alleged conscious parallel conduct. It found no plausibility. "Without more," the Court reasoned, "parallel conduct does not suggest conspiracy … . [W]hen allegations of parallel conduct are set out in order to make a [conspiracy] claim, they must be placed in a context that raises a suggestion of a preceding agreement."[151]

167. Three years later, the Court reaffirmed *Twombly* in *Ashcroft v. Iqbal.*[152] Iqbal, a citizen of Pakistan and a Muslim, was detained under harsh conditions in the wake of the September 11 attacks. He sued John Ashcroft, the U.S. Attorney General, and Robert Mueller, the F.B.I. Director, alleging that Ashcroft was the principal architect of, and that Mueller was instrumental in, the deployment of a detention policy that intentionally targeted Muslims and citizens of Muslim countries. To prove his claim, Iqbal would have to show that Ashcroft and Mueller personally and intentionally discriminated against him based on his race, religion, or national origin, and Iqbal argued that that conclusion was plausible in light of his allegations. The Supreme Court disagreed. Applying *Twombly*, the Court disregarded Iqbal's allegations of the defendants' involvement in the policy as legal conclusions rather than direct factual allegations and then concluded that his remaining factual allegations, though consistent with intentional discrimination, did not plausibly suggest intentional discrimination by the defendants in light of more likely lawful explanations for the conduct. The Court explained that judges to assess plausibility in light of "judicial experience and common sense."[153]

149. 550 U.S. 544 (2007).
150. *Ibid.*, at 560–563.
151. *Ibid.*, at 556–557.
152. 556 U.S. 662 (2009).
153. *Ibid.*, at 678–683.

168. Assessing a motion to dismiss under Rule 12(b)(6) now has two steps. First, the complaint must be *legally sufficient* in that it pursues a claim that the law recognizes. Second, the complaint must be *factually sufficient.* In evaluating factual sufficiency, courts should disregard any conclusory allegations and then determine, using judicial experience and common sense, whether the remaining factual allegations state a plausible claim.

II. Answer

169. If the defendant forgoes a preanswer motion, or if the case is not fully dismissed after a preanswer motion, the defendant must answer the complaint. If a preanswer motion was filed, the defendant normally has fourteen days from the court's decision on the motion to file an answer; absent a preanswer motion, the defendant has twenty-one days from service—or sixty days from waiver of service—to file the answer.[154]

170. The purposes of the answer are to isolate what allegations in the plaintiff's complaint the defendant disputes and to provide notice of any defenses or affirmative claims the defendant asserts in the case. The answer contains up to three main parts: responses to the complaint's allegations, assertions of defenses, and allegations of the defendant's own affirmative claims against the plaintiff, other parties, or third parties. The first two parts will be discussed in the immediately following paragraphs; joinder of claims and parties will be discussed in the separate section below on joinder.

171. All answers must respond to the complaint by admitting or denying each allegation. If the defendant lacks sufficient information to either admit or deny an allegation, the defendant can so state, which has the effect of a denial. If a paragraph of the complaint can be neither wholly admitted nor wholly denied, the answer must admit the admittable part and deny the rest. Any allegation not denied is deemed admitted.[155] The point of forcing the defendant to respond to each allegation is to isolate matters of dispute and agreement between the parties. Matters admitted need not be proved at trial. Accordingly, the answer helps clarify what issues must be litigated.

172. Affirmative defenses are contentions of fact or law that avoid liability even if the plaintiff otherwise proves the claim. Generally speaking, a defendant bears the burden of persuasion at trial on any matter constituting an affirmative defense. Such defenses include expiration of the statute of limitations, preclusion of the plaintiff's claim, waiver of the plaintiff's claim, and contributory negligence on the part of the plaintiff. Rule 8(c) requires that the defendant "affirmatively state any avoidance or affirmative defense." If an affirmative defense is not specifically included in the

154. Fed. R. Civ. P. 12(a).
155. Fed. R. Civ. P. 8(b).

defendant's answer, the defendant waives the defense and is not permitted to introduce evidence at trial regarding the waived defense.

173. In addition, the defendant can assert the defenses listed in Rule 12(b) in the answer. However, the defenses of lack of personal jurisdiction, improper venue, insufficient service of process, and insufficient service must be raised in the defendant's first responsive filing—whether preanswer motion or answer—or they are waived. Thus, if the defendant filed a preanswer motion asserting only a lack of personal jurisdiction, the defendant has waived the defenses based on venue and service and can no longer assert them in the answer.[156]

174. If the complaint and answer (together, "the pleadings") establish either the plaintiff's claim to relief (such as if the defendant admits all the facts establishing the defendant's liability to the plaintiff) or the defendant's avoidance of the claim by defense (such as if the pleadings show the plaintiff's untimeliness under an applicable limitations period), a party may file a motion for judgment on the pleadings, and the court can grant the motion and issue judgment to the prevailing party.[157]

§4. Sanctions

I. Rule 11

175. The strictures of Rule 11 apply to all pleadings and motions, as well as other papers filed with the court. The rule states that the attorney or party signing the filed paper "certifies that to the best of the person's knowledge, information, and belief, formed after an inquiry reasonable under the circumstances: (1) it is not being presented for any improper purpose, such as to harass, cause unnecessary delay, or needlessly increase the cost of litigation; (2) the claims, defenses, and other legal contentions are warraned by existing law or by a nonfrivolous argument for extending, modifying, or reversing existing law or for establishing new law; (3) the factual contentions have evidentiary support or, if specifically so identified, will likely have evidentiary support after ar easonable opportunity for further investigation or discovery; and (4) the denials of factual contentions are warranted on the evidence or, if specifically so identified, are reasonably based on belief of a lack of information."[158]

176. If a violation of Rule 11 is suspected by a party, the party can serve a motion for sanctions on the suspected violator but may not file the motion with the court if the violation is corrected within twenty-one days after service of the motion. If the court suspects a violation on its own, the court can order the suspected violator to show cause why a sanction should not be imposed.[159]

156. Fed. R. Civ. P. 12(h).
157. Fed. R. Civ. P. 12(c).
158. Fed. R. Civ. P. 11(b).
159. Fed. R. Civ. P. 11(c).

177. If the court, after notice and an opportunity for the violator to be heard, finds a violation, the court may impose an appropriate sanction. If the violator is an attorney, the attorney's firm is jointly responsible for the violation.[160] The sanction must be limited to what suffices to deter repetition of the conduct by the violator or others similarly situated. The sanction may take the form of nonmonetary directives, a monetary penalty, or fee shifting.[161]

II. Inherent Power

178. The U.S. Supreme Court has held that federal courts have inherent power to control the conduct in their courtroom and in their cases. This inherent power includes the contempt power, which often takes the form of monetary sanctions or attorney-fee shifting to sanction misconduct. The inherent sanctioning power is broader than Rule 11 in that it applies to all conduct, not just representations in written filings. In *Chambers v. NASCO, Inc.*,[162] the U.S. Supreme Court held that a federal court's inherent sanctioning power is not necessarily a last resort and may be deployed as an alternative to sanctions under Rule 11. This power may be exercised against a prevailing as well as a losing party and is justified if the sanctionable conduct was undertaken in bad faith, even if the rest of the litigation was otherwise conducted in good faith.

§5. Amending Pleadings

179. The purpose of pleadings is to identify the issues in dispute, but as the case progresses, some issues may no longer be in dispute, while other issues may suddenly present themselves as a litigable dispute. Even whole claims and defenses may change. The American approach is to be flexible to allow disputes to be resolved according to the facts, not according to what the parties *think* the dispute is about at the time of filing. Consequently, the Federal Rules adopt a flexible mode of amending pleadings as the case develops.

180. A party can amend their pleading once as a matter of course—without needing consent of another party or the court—by filing the amendment no later than twenty-one days after service of the answer.[163] This is essentially a free opportunity to amend, though it must be done at a very early stage. This kind of amendment typically corrects mistakes or oversights in the original pleading. In all other cases, a party may amend their pleading only with the opposing party's consent or the court's leave, but the court will freely give leave when justice so requires.[164] In practice, justice usually will permit amendment—because of the preference for

160. Fed. R. Civ. P. 11(c)(1).
161. Fed. R. Civ. P. 11(c)(4).
162. 501 U.S. 32 (1991).
163. Fed. R. Civ. P. 15(a)(1).
164. Fed. R. Civ. P. 15(a)(2).

framing cases according to the facts as they are uncovered—unless the amending party has acted in bad faith or the opponent will be prejudiced in their ability to litigate the amended issues. As long as the party acts in good faith, the party can add or drop claims, defenses, or parties, change factual allegations, or change admissions to denials or vice versa. Again, the liberal approach to amendments is grounded in the goal of freeing parties to have their dispute decided according to the information relevant to the case as it unfolds rather than hamstring the parties to positions they articulated without full information.

181. An amended pleading that adds new claims or new defendants presents a special problem if the applicable limitations period has run between the date of the original pleading and the date of the amended pleading. Rule 15 tries to balance the defendant's need for repose with the plaintiff's need for justice. If the amendment asserts a claim or defense that arose out of the same conduct, transaction, or occurrence set out in the original pleading, then the amendment will "relate back" and be deemed to have been filed as of the date of the original pleading for purposes of any limitations period. After all, if the defendant is already being sued by the plaintiff for claims arising from an incident, the defendant has less justification for repose if the plaintiff adds a new, but now untimely, claim arising from the same incident. If the amendment adds a new defendant, however, then the amendment will relate back only if the claim against the new defendant relates back and only if the new defendant, within ninety days of the filing of the original pleading, received notice of the action and knew or should have known that they should have been named as a defendant in the original pleading but for a mistake concerning the identity of the proper defendant.[165]

165. Fed. R. Civ. P. 15(c).

Chapter 2. Joinder and Class Actions

182. The federal courts and most state courts encourage the aggregation of multiple claims and parties in a single civil action. Aggregation enhances judicial economy by avoiding an unnecessary multiplicity of litigation, and it reduces the possibility of separate courts entering inconsistent judgments. This chapter discusses claim joinder, party joinder, consolidation, and class actions.

183. In general, joinder requires both authorization under the Federal Rules and jurisdiction. The rules do not speak to jurisdiction; the jurisdictional analysis must be undertaken pursuant to separate and independent jurisdictional principles, such as diversity jurisdiction and supplemental jurisdiction, discussed above in Chapter 1. This Chapter focuses on rule authorization.

§1. Claim Joinder

184. Say an Iowa farmer purchases a tractor from the tractor manufacturer, a company incorporated in Delaware with its headquarters in Delaware. The tractor malfunctions and injures the farmer. The farmer sues the manufacturer in federal court for product liability, a common tort claim, for compensation for injuries exceeding USD 75,000. Say the farmer also had purchased tractor oil from the tractor manufacturer, but the manufacturer failed to ship the oil to the farmer. The farmer has a breach of contract claim against the manufacturer for failing to ship the oil. Can the farmer add the contract claim to the tort case so that they can be litigated together? Say also the farmer, understandably upset at the manufacturer, posts libelous statements about the manufacturer on social media. The manufacturer wishes to assert a claim against the farmer for libel. Can the manufacturer do so in the farmer's lawsuit? The answer to both questions is yes.

185. Rule 18 provides that once a claimant asserts a claim against an opponent, the claimant may assert all other claims that claimant has against that opponent, even if the claims are unrelated to each other.[166] And Rule 13 provides that the opponent may assert all claims the opponent has against the original claimant, even if unrelated.[167] The rationale is that once the parties are both before a court in an adversarial posture, they should litigate all their disputes in a single proceeding.

186. The rule for the opponent's claims against the original claimant—called counterclaims—has a wrinkle. For counterclaims that are related to the original claim, the efficiency gains of litigating those together are too great to pass up. Accordingly, Rule 13 makes related counterclaims compulsory—the opponent must assert them in the claimant's lawsuit or be barred from asserting them elsewhere.[168]

166. Fed. R. Civ. P. 18(a).
167. Fed. R. Civ. P. 13(a)–(b).
168. Fed. R. Civ. P. 13(a). The compulsion does not apply if the court cannot obtain jurisdiction over the claim or party. *Ibid.*

187. If the plaintiff sues two defendants, a defendant may assert a claim against the other defendant—called a cross-claim—in the same lawsuit, but only if the cross-claim is related to the plaintiff's original claim.[169] The rationale is that a related cross-claim has sufficient efficiency justification for hearing it with the original claim, but the option to assert it is at the whim of the defendant, who may not wish to bring the claim in the plaintiff's chosen forum. An unrelated cross-claim provides no efficiency gains, and so allowing it would only serve to detract from (and make more expensive and involved) the plaintiff's original lawsuit. The same rules apply to cross-claims between co-plaintiffs.

188. If claim joinder presents a risk of complexity or confusion, the court has discretion to order separate trials on claims to avoid prejudice or to expedite or economize the litigation.[170]

§2. Party Joinder

I. Juridical Capacity and Real Party in Interest

189. Juridical capacity—the capacity to sue or be sued—is a prerequisite for a person or entity to be party to a civil action. And when a party with juridical capacity purports to represent the interests of some other person or entity, issues of whether the "real party in interest" should be joined to the litigation may arise.

190. In federal practice, issues of "real party in interest" status and juridical capacity are governed by Rule 17 of the Federal Rules of Civil Procedure. The rule sets forth a list of common types of representative parties, such as executors, trustees of express trusts, and parties otherwise statutorily authorized to sue for the benefit of others, and empowers them to proceed with litigation without joinder of those whose interests they represent. In other situations, the rule provides liberally that representative litigation may proceed if within a reasonable time after an objection is raised by a "real party in interest," the defect is cured by ratification of the litigation by the real party in interest, or by joinder or substitution of the real party in interest on a "nunc pro tunc" basis (now for then) that treats the newly added real party in interest as having been joined from the outset of the litigation. This allows "real party in interest" problems to be cured even when the applicable statute of limitations would bar the commencement of new litigation brought by the real party in interest. Nonetheless, the determination that an absentee is a real party in interest may sometimes require dismissal of a federal civil action if the real party in interest's citizenship destroys the diversity of citizenship upon which federal jurisdiction depends.[171]

---

169. Fed. R. Civ. P. 13(g).
170. Fed. R. Civ. P. 42(b).
171. Fed. R. Civ. P. 17(a).

191. Rule 17 also provides that the juridical capacity of an individual or corporation generally is to be determined by reference to the law of the state in which the individual is domiciled or the corporation was organized. In other cases (those involving unincorporated associations and parties acting in a representative capacity), juridical capacity is determined by reference to the law of the state in which the federal district court is located. Notwithstanding any contrary state law, however, partnerships and unincorporated associations (typically labor unions) have the capacity to sue and be sued in federal court in order to enforce a substantive right granted by federal law in favor of, or against, such an entity. Federal law also governs the juridical capacity of receivers appointed by federal courts to hold and manage property.[172]

192. The rule provides that suits by or against a minor or incompetent are maintainable by a previously appointed fiduciary or specially appointed guardian ad litem.[173]

193. A final requirement imposed on a party seeking to prosecute a civil action is that the party have "standing" to sue. As a matter of state law, "standing" issues are generally subsumed within the law of juridical capacity and "real party in interest" status. In the federal courts, however, "standing" issues have an added jurisdictional dimension that is discussed in detail in the next subsection.

II. Permissive Joinder

194. Plaintiffs may join together as co-plaintiffs and may join multiple defendants together as co-defendants, if the claims uniting the co-parties: (a) arise out of the same transaction, occurrence, or series of transactions or occurrences and (b) entail a common question of law or fact.[174] Again, the rationale is to promote the benefits of aggregation: if claims against or by different parties are related, joinder should enhance efficiency. If confusion or embarrassment or inefficiences result, the court has discretion to hold separate trials or issue other orders to protect against those effects.[175] If a party is improperly joined, the court can drop the party or sever the claim without having to dismiss other claims and parties properly joined.[176]

195. Although party joinder generally enhances efficiency, it often involves significantly more complexity and expense than claim joinder. Accordingly, most party joinder is permissive—at the option of the claimant. The permissive nature of party joinder induces strategic decision-making. Often, multiple plaintiffs wish to join together to gain the advantages of economies of scale, to pool and share resources, and to signal a show of strength or widespread harm. Plaintiffs also often prefer to

172. Fed. R. Civ. P. 17(b).
173. Fed. R. Civ. P. 17(c).
174. Fed. R. Civ. P. 20(a).
175. Fed. R. Civ. P. 20(b); Fed. R. Civ. P. 42(b).
176. Fed. R. Civ. P. 21.

join defendants so that, if the defendants point the figure at each other, the plaintiffs can assure themselves that some defendant will be found liable. But, in other cases, plaintiffs may prefer to litigate individually or may prefer to sue defendants separately. The permissive-joinder rules provide room for such strategic decision-making.

III. Required Joinder

196. Although most party joinder is permissive, the Federal Rules recognize that the exclusion of a nonparty may be so prejudicial to that nonparty's interests that exclusion violates fundamental fairness and justice. If, for example, the nonparty's absence prevents the court from awarding complete relief to the existing parties, or the nonparty claims an interest that would be impaired or impeded by the nonparty's absence, or an existing party may be subject to excessive or inconsistent obligations without the nonparty's participation, then the nonparty is required to be joined if feasible under service rules and jurisdictional doctrines.[177] The court will join the nonparty over the existing parties' and even over the nonparty's objections. If the nonparty is aligned with the plaintiff, the nonparty will be made an involuntary plaintiff.[178]

197. Required joinder arises infrequently, but a classic circumstance justifying required joinder is co-ownership of property. Say Jane and Joy jointly hold a patent. A licensee sues Joy, arguing that the patent is invalid. Jane's own interest in the patent may be extinguished by the litigation even though she has not been named as a party. She should be joined to the lawsuit as a required party so that her interest will not be adjudicated in her absence.

198. If the required nonparty cannot be joined because of service or jurisdictional problems, then the court must determine whether, "in equity and good conscience," the action should continue without the nonparty or be wholly dismissed.[179]

IV. Interpleader

199. Interpleader is a specialized form of required joinder of parties. It is used by a party (the "stakeholder") in possession of property (the "stake") to which two or more (often many more) parties have or may assert conflicting claims. The classic circumstance involves an insurer who must pay out on an insurance claim, but multiple purported beneficiaries claim entitlement to the same payout. In that circumstance, each beneficiary could initiate an individual action, and the insurer thus

177. Fed. R. Civ. P. 19(a)(1).
178. Fed. R. Civ. P. 19(a)(2).
179. Fed. R. Civ. P. 19(b).

could face multiple judgments to pay the same benefit.[180] To avoid this unfairness, interpleader allows the insurer (the stakeholder) to initiate an impleader action by joining all rival claimants in one lawsuit to resolve how the single benefit is to be awarded.[181]

200. To facilitate required joinder in interpleader when the claims arise under state law and involve some parties from the same state and other parties from other states, Congress has, by special statutory provisions, provided for federal subject-matter jurisdiction based on minimal diversity[182] and has supplied federal courts with nationwide personal jurisdiction.[183]

V. Intervention

201. In some cases, a nonparty may have an interest in the litigation that it desires to protect by becoming a party to the litigation. The Federal Rules broadly authorize the joinder of third parties at their own request—also called "intervention."[184] Intervention services to broaden the participation of parties with various interests in the litigation, which is especially important for American litigation, which often involves matters of broad public interest. Intervention comes in two forms: of right and permissive.

202. Intervention of right requires the trial court to grant a timely motion to intervene if the proposed intervenor has been granted a right to intervene by statute or, more typically, "when the applicant claims an interest relating to the property or transaction that is the subject of the action, and is so situated that, disposing of the action may as a practical matter impair or impede the movant's ability to protect its interest, unless existing parties adequately represent that interest."[185] This latter form of intervention of right can be seen as a complement to required joinder.

203. A nonparty that lacks the qualifications for intervention of right may nevertheless seek to intervene permissively if a federal statute confers a conditional right to intervene or the nonparty has a claim or defense that shares with the main action a common question of law or fact.[186] Unlike other permissive joinder, permissive intervention is subject to court discretion. The court must weigh the benefit of intervention against the costs of intervention, and permissive intervention will only be allowed with court approval.

180. *See, e.g., State Farm Fire & Casualty Co. v. Tashire*, 386 U.S. 523 (1967).
181. Fed. R. Civ. P. 22.
182. 28 U.S.C. §1335.
183. 28 U.S.C. §2361.
184. Fed. R. Civ. P. 24.
185. Fed. R. Civ. P. 24(a).
186. Fed. R. Civ. P. 24(b).

VI. Impleader

204. A party threatened with liability may have a claim for insurance, indemnification, or contribution against a nonparty who may be responsible for the party's liability. The classic example is a liability-insurance arrangement in which the insured is personally liable but the insurance policy contractually obligates the insurer to pay any damages—and even to defend the insurer in the litigation. Other examples depend upon other kinds of contractual arrangements for indemnification or upon contribution under American tort law, which usually allows for claims among multiple tortfeasors to allocate liability according to proportionate fault.

205. If a nonparty is ultimately liable for insurance coverage, indemnification, or contribution, a party facing liability can join the nonparty in a process called impleader. The existing party files and serves a third-party complaint against the nonparty, who then is joined as a third-party defendant to the impleader claim.[187] Once joined, the third-party defendant can assert counterclaims against the third-party plaintiff who initiated the impleader on the same terms as otherwise applicable under the counterclaim rule, can assert related claims against the original plaintiff, and can even assert defenses formally held by the third-party plaintiff against the original plaintiff's claims.[188] The latter right is necessitated by the risk that a defendant who knows they will be fully covered for any liability refuses to vigorously defend against liability. The original plaintiff may, once the third-party defendant has been impleaded, assert any related claim against the third-party defendant.[189]

§3. Consolidation

206. Whole cases can be "joined" together in a process called consolidation. If separate actions before a single court involve a common question of law or fact, the court may consolidate the actions to be heard in consolidated fashion before a single judge.[190] Consolidation can prove beneficial for reasons similar to claim and party joinder.

207. A specialized form of consolidation called multidistrict litigation, also discussed above in Part II, Chapter II, is widely used to aggregate geographically dispersed cases involving, primarily, mass torts. A medical device, for example, may affect thousands, perhaps tens of thousands, of individual plaintiffs, each of whom may individually sue the single manufacturer in various federal courts around the country. Each of these individual lawsuits can involve very similar questions of law and fact bearing on the manufacturer's liability. The multidistrict-litigation statute

187. Fed. R. Civ. P. 14(a).
188. Fed. R. Civ. P. 14(a)(2).
189. Fed. R. Civ. P. 14(a)(3).
190. Fed. R. Civ. P. 42(a).

enables the transfer of each case from its original court of filing to a single, designated federal court for consolidated pretrial matters.[191] At the conclusion of consolidated pretrial matters, the designated court must remand each case back to its original court for trial.[192] In practice, consolidated litigation often resolves individual cases through dismissal, summary judgment, or settlement. Multidistrict litigation has proven to be highly efficient at resolving disputes, though the efficiency comes with the costs of rough justice and of incursions on the autonomy of plaintiffs to control their cases.

§4. Class Actions

I. Background

208. The claim joinder, party joinder, and consolidation discussed above all involve parties representing themselves in the litigation. Class actions are different because they involve named representatives litigating on behalf of a multitude of others who have limited rights to participate in the litigation. The vast majority of class actions are brought by plaintiff classes, so this section will focus on plaintiff classes.

209. A typical class action is commenced by one or more "named" plaintiffs who sue one or more defendants on behalf of a group of similarly wronged persons too numerous to permit these additional plaintiffs to be joined in an individual capacity. Class actions offer many advantages. First, they offer many of the same advantages as ordinary joinder—efficiency and the avoidance of inconsistent judgments. Second, they enable the pooling of litigation resources on such a broad scale as to enable very small-value claims to be litigated in the first place. Few plaintiffs would sue individually over a USD 5 claim for, say, an excessive fee imposed by a cell phone company. And certainly, no lawyer would take that claim. Yet the cell phone company would be enriched to the tune of many millions of dollars. Class actions enable all class members to litigate their claims as a unit—if the class contains a million consumers who each suffered USD 5 in excessive fees, the class claims total USD 5 million, making the litigation economically viable and attractive for legal representation.

210. But class actions, as representative litigation, also come with significant risks. Class members are not formal parties to the action—only the named representatives are formal parties for their individual claims, and the class as a whole is the party for the class claims. Unnamed class members' legal rights are at stake because classwide resolution will adjudicate their claims, but they have no right to participate in discovery or file motions or advance their claims individually unless they formally intervene as an individual party. The named representatives and class counsel represent the class as a whole for the benefit of the class members.

191. 28 U.S.C. §1407.
192. *Lexecon, Inc. v. Milberg Weiss Bershad Hynes & Lerach*, 523 U.S. 26 (1998).

211. The representational nature of class actions thus presents the real risk that the named representatives and class counsel will not vigorously litigate all class members' interests equally. Say, for example, a class of drivers sues a tire manufacturer for injuries when the manufactured tire malfunctions. The named representatives might have substantial physical injuries but, because of their circumstances, very modest lost wages or emotional damages. The named representatives might proceed in the litigation to maximize recovery for physical injuries at the expense of full recovery for other types of damages, even though some class members may have the opposite interest.

212. Further, because class counsel are often compensated based on contingency fees calculated as a percentage of the benefit awarded to the class, class counsel may attempt to settle the case on terms most favorable to attorneys fees and less favorable to class members. A cell phone company might, for example, agree to a settlement in which each class member is given a voucher for USD 5 off their next bill, but the voucher must be redeemed by some affirmative conduct by the individual consumer. Class counsel may seek a contingency fee based on an asserted USD 5 million in voucher benefits to the class even though, as a practical matter, far fewer than all class members will take the step to redeem a USD 5 voucher.

II. Prerequisites

213. Because of these risks, the Federal Rules create special rules to ensure that class actions will serve the efficiency role they are geared for in ways that protect the rights of absent class members. Rule 23(a) sets out four prerequisites for treatment as a class action: numerosity, commonality, typicality, and adequacy.[193]

214. The numerosity prerequisite requires that the number of class members be so numerous that ordinary joinder is impracticable. The threshold number varies from court to court and class to class but generally is between forty and one hundred class members. This prerequisite helps to ensure that the class action is really an appropriate alternative to individualized litigation.

215. The commonality prerequisite requires that all class members' claims share at least one common question of law or fact. Although this requirement was normally thought to be easily met, the U.S. Supreme Court, in *Wal-Mart Stores, Inc. v. Dukes*,[194] held that a class of female employees of Wal-Mart did not meet the commonality requirement in their claims of sex discrimination in promotions. The Court held that commonality requires that each class member has suffered the same injury and that the common question must be one that produces a common answer that will advance or stymie all class claims in the same way.[195] This requirement ensures that sufficient efficiencies will justify the representative nature of the class action.

---

193. Fed. R. Civ. P. 23(a).
194. 564 U.S. 338 (2011).
195. *Ibid.,* at 350.

216. The typicality prerequisite demands that the named party have claims or defenses typical of the class. If the class representative does not have the same claims or the same kinds of damages, or if the representative's claim is subject to different defenses, then the representative is not typical. For example, a class representative who asserts a claim for race discrimination in promotions cannot represent those who have claims for race discrimination in hiring.[196] This prerequisite helps to ensure alignment of legal interests between the representative and the class to enhance the representational quality of the class action.

217. The adequacy prerequisite parallels the typicality requirement but focuses on the capacity rather than the interests of the representative party in asking whether the representative party is likely to be able to fairly and adequately protect the interests of the class. Perhaps the class representative cannot give the litigation sufficient attention or otherwise would be a poor agent for advancing the class's interests. This prerequisite helps to ensure a zealous representation of the class.

III. Types

218. If all four prerequisites are met, the class may be maintained if it meets the requirements of one of three types of class actions.[197] The first is the so-called mandatory class, in which individualized litigation would prejudice either the defendant or the class members. This type of class reflects the same motivations as required joinder and interpleader, though it is decidedly rare in class-action form.

219. The second type of class action applies when the defendant has acted or refused to act on grounds that apply generally to the class such that injunctive or declaratory relief is appropriate, respecting the class as a whole. The classic example of this type of class is a class that seeks injunctive relief to end discriminatory conduct directed at a class of people who share the characteristic being discriminated against. The famous desegregation case of *Brown v. Board of Education* falls within this type of class action.[198] If the class seeks monetary relief that is not incidental to the injunctive relief, however, the class cannot be maintained under this type.[199]

220. The third type is a catch-all type in which the claims do not so clearly lend themselves to class treatment. This third type requires that the common questions "predominate" over individual questions and that the class action is the "superior" method for fairly and efficiently adjudicating the controversy. Today, most class actions—securities, antitrust, civil rights, consumer rights, and mass torts, just to name a few—are pursued under this type, which allows for significant monetary damages.

196. *General Telephone Co. of Southwest v. Falcon*, 457 U.S. 147, 157–158 (1982).
197. Fed. R. Civ. P. 23(b).
198. 347 U.S. 483 (1954).
199. *Wal-Mart Stores*, 564 U.S. at 360.

IV. Certification, Counsel, and Notice

221. The judge makes the determination as to whether to "certify" the action as a class action because all the requirements are met.[200] The prerequisites of Rule 23 and the factors supporting the maintenance of a class as one of the three specified types are not mere pleading standards based on allegations but rather require "significant proof" to convince a court that they are met after a "rigorous analysis."[201]

222. If the court certifies the class, it must define the class in a written order. The court also must appoint class counsel. Unlike ordinary litigation, in which a party can hire an attorney of their choice or even no attorney at all, the court must appoint class counsel and must take into account class counsel's experience, knowledge, and resources.[202] The court serves as gatekeeper to help ensure that the class will be well represented by counsel.

223. Upon certification, the court must provide notice to all class members if the class is certified under the third type of class action. The court may provide notice to class members if the class is certified under another type. The notice must be in plain, ordinary language and describe the nature of the action, the definition of the class, the class claims, the right to intervene, and the binding nature of the class action on individual class-member rights.[203]

224. In the third type of class action, the notice also must give class members the right to opt out of the class. A class member who timely opts out will no longer be bound by the class outcome and instead retain their individual right to pursue the claim.[204] In practice, very few class members ever opt-out.

225. After certification, the court maintains authority to oversee the class litigation to ensure that the class is being represented fairly and adequately and that the litigation is proceeding expeditiously.[205] Typically, courts maintain close control of the litigation, such that class litigation is far more judge-directed than nonclass litigation.

V. Settlement

226. Settlement presents special concerns of faithful agency because, at the time of settlement, class counsel is negotiating a conclusion to the litigation with the

200. Fed. R. Civ. P. 23(c)(1).
201. *Wal-Mart Stores*, 564 U.S. at 350–351.
202. Fed. R. Civ. P. 23(c)(1), 23(g)(1).
203. Fed. R. Civ. P. 23(c)(2).
204. Fed. R. Civ. P. 23(c)(2).
205. Fed. R. Civ. P. 23(d).

defendant, and the absent class members are not present. The protections in the Federal Rules demand "heightened scrutiny" at settlement,[206] and the rules specify that the action cannot be settled without the approval of the court.[207] This requirement is a marked difference from nonclass litigation, in which the parties generally can settle on any terms they wish, without even having to inform the court of those terms.

227. Class actions, by contrast, may be settled only with court approval after an additional set of requirements. First, the court usually will give notice to the class members of the settlement and its terms. The notice usually will give each class member a right to opt out of the settlement or to object to the settlement. Second, the court will hold a public hearing in which objectors may voice objections to the settlement. Third, the court will approve a binding settlement only after finding that the settlement is fair, reasonable, and adequate.

VI. Distribution and Conclusion

228. After settlement or judgment in favor of the class, the court retains jurisdiction to oversee the distribution of relief to the class members on an equitable basis. For a cash settlement, the defendant usually deposits the funds and exits the litigation, leaving class counsel and the court to oversee equitable distribution. Often, the court will appoint a vendor to administer the class award, including giving notice to class members about how to file a claim for individual relief, evaluating the claims, and ensuring payment.

229. The court also approves any attorney fee paid to class counsel. Courts often scrutinize the fee to ensure that it is reasonable in light of the class recovery and the effort expended by counsel.

206. *Ortiz v. Fibreboard Corp.*, 527 U.S. 815 (1999); *Amchem Products, Inc. v. Windsor*, 521 U.S. 591 (1997).
207. Fed. R. Civ. P. 23(e).

Chapter 3. Case Management

230. Although the American style of civil litigation generally relies on the parties to steer the case, federal judges have extensive managerial powers and broad discretion to use them. This Chapter briefly discusses those managerial powers.

§1. Managerial Authority

231. Courts must issue a scheduling order soon after the answer is filed. The purpose of the order is to set deadlines for pretrial matters such as discovery and motions for summary judgment and set a trial date.[208]

232. In addition, the Federal Rules give courts power to order the attorneys to attend a pretrial conference to discuss expediting the action, discouraging waste, improving preparation and participation, and facilitating settlement.[209] At a pretrial conference, the court can narrow the issues in contention, eliminate nonmeritorious claims or defenses, obtain admissions and stipulations about facts otherwise in dispute, invite amendments and motions, and adopt other procedures. Party violation of managerial directives can result in sanctions.[210] Use of managerial powers varies depending upon the nature of the case and sophistication and antagonism of the parties, but a judge occasionally will set a monthly standing pretrial conference in a complex or adversarial case to keep the parties on track.

233. Controversially, the managerial powers include the power to encourage settlement.[211] Such facilitation can take the form of commenting on the merits of the parties' positions, staying discovery or postponing trial to give parties time to negotiate or mediate, or referring the case to mediation. Judges cannot force a settlement, but strong signaling can induce the parties to the bargaining table. That said, many judges shy away from heavyhanded approaches to settlement encouragement.

§2. Use of Adjuncts

234. A federal judge can refer matters to court adjuncts such as special masters or magistrate judges.[212] Magistrate judges are not judges appointed through the constitutional process but rather are judicial employees authorized by statute and appointed by the district court to eight-year terms.[213] Magistrate judges exercise

208. Fed. R. Civ. P. 16(b).
209. Fed. R. Civ. P. 16(a), (c).
210. Fed. R. Civ. P. 16(f).
211. Fed. R. Civ. P. 16(a)(5).
212. Fed. R. Civ. P. 16(c)(2)(H).
213. 28 U.S.C. §631.

judicial power only as authorized by federal statute generally and by the district judge or by consent of the parties in a particular case.[214]

235. A district judge can refer a nondispositive matter to the magistrate judge assigned to the case. The magistrate judge can issue a written ruling to which the parties can object, and the district judge then can modify or set aside any part of the order that is clearly erroneous or contrary to law.[215] Nondispositive matters routinely decided by magistrate judges include discovery disputes, motions to amend, and the like.

236. A district judge can refer a dispositive matter to the magistrate judge assigned to the case. The magistrate judge may hold a hearing and otherwise develop the necessary record and then must issue a recommended disposition to the district judge. A party can file objections to the recommendation, which the district judge must consider. The district judge then must review any matter objected to de novo. The district judge may accept, reject, or modify the recommendation in its own dispositive order, may receive further evidence, or may return the matter to the magistrate judge with instructions.[216]

237. Magistrate judges may conduct any civil proceding, including a trial, by consent of all parties.[217] Judgments entered by a magistrate judge by consent of the parties are final and not reviewed by the district judge but may be appealed to the intermediate Court of Appeals.[218]

214. 28 U.S.C. §636.
215. Fed. R. Civ. P. 72(a).
216. Fed. R. Civ. P. 72(b).
217. Fed. R. Civ. P. 73(a).
218. Fed. R. Civ. P. 73(c).

Chapter 4. Discovery

§1. Scope of Discovery

238. Discovery is the formal process by which parties obtain information from their adversaries or other witnesses who may have information bearing on the litigation. Discovery in an adversarial system initially seems anomalous, like if poker players had to show their cards in the middle of the hand. But the American approach recognizes, as all systems recognize, that truth requires disclosure. In the Supreme Court's words, discovery aims to "make a trial less a game of blind man's bluff and more a fair contest with the basic issues and the facts disclosed to the fullest practicable extent."[219] U.S. discovery remains adversarial in that it is directed by parties rather than the judge. In other words, the parties make requests and disclosures on their own, without involving the judge or filing the requests or disclosures with the court. The judge often enters the discovery process only to decide a motion filed by one of the parties to resolve a discovery dispute.

239. Because the pleadings are based on unverified allegations, require no contemporaneous submission of evidence, and permit alternative or even speculative assertions, broad discovery is necessary to weed out contentions that lack evidentiary support and to provide a basis for resolving factual disputes by the judge or jury. Discovery thus is designed to serve a number of related purposes. It enables parties to find out information necessary to prepare for trial, helps narrow the issues in the case by eliminating from the litigation those issues that are not contested, produces a record and locks parties into certain positions so that opposing parties do not face moving targets later in litigation, and preserves information that may be used directly at trial if the source of the information is no longer available at the time of trial.

240. Under the American rule of cost and fee allocation, each party bears its own costs to request or produce discovery. And broad discovery means costly discovery. Discovery is usually the costliest phase of litigation. The Federal Rules thus try to balance the need for discovery against the costs of discovery.

241. Matters are discoverable if they are relevant to a claim or defense asserted in the pleadings, nonprivileged, and proportional to the needs of the case. The information need not be admissible into evidence to be discoverable. Proportionality is assessed under the following considerations: the importance of the issues at stake in the action, the amount of controversy, the parties' relative access to relevant information, the parties' resources, the importance of the discovery in resolving the issues, and whether the burden or expense of the proposed discovery outweighs its likely benefit.[220] Privileges are discussed below.

---

219. *United States v. Procter & Gamble Co.*, 356 U.S. 677, 682–683 (1958).
220. Fed. R. Civ. P. 26(b)(1).

242. Even when within the scope of discovery, the judge can issue an order protecting a party from having to produce information if the request is unreasonably cumulative or duplicative or can be obtained from another source that is more convenient or less burdensome or less expensive, or if the requesting party had ample opportunity to obtain the information in previous discovery requests.[221] In addition, a party need not produce otherwise discoverable electronically stored information if the information is not "reasonably accessible because of undue burden or cost."[222]

243. Disputes about whether the requested information is within the scope of discovery arise frequently, in part because the requesting party often does not know what information is in the hands of the opponent. When a responding party believes the information requested falls outside the scope of discovery, the responding party will object to the request and state the grounds for the request. If the requesting party wishes to challenge the objection and withholding, the requesting party will initiate a meet-and-confer conversation in which the parties explore options for resolving the dispute. Options may include rephrasing the request, narrowing the request, agreeing upon the use of search terms, redacting information, delaying discovery, and the like. If the parties cannot resolve their disagreement on their own, either the requesting party will file a motion to compel, or the responding party will file a motion for a protective order. The judge will then decide whether and on what terms the discovery must be produced.

244. A special but ubiquitous type of protective order is colloquially called a confidentiality order. Normally, no restrictions apply to the sharing of information, but because disclosing embarrassing, private, or proprietary information can be burdensome, a judge will often, as stipulated by the parties, issue an order setting guidelines about and limits on how information exchanged in discovery can be disseminated or shared. Confidentiality orders have proven particularly useful tools in facilitating the safe exchange of information, though at the expense of public awareness of litigation matters of broad concern.

245. To help stave off disputes, the Federal Rules require the parties to hold an initial conference to jointly develop a discovery plan that makes arrangements for the amount, extent, timing, and other conditions of discovery requests and responses. The parties then submit the plan to the court, which approves it as a court order. Any disagreements noted by the parties in the plan are resolved by the judge in the order.[223]

§2. Privileges and Work Product

246. State privilege law governs privileges applicable to state-law claims and defenses, while federal privilege law (including federal common law) governs

221. Fed. R. Civ. P. 26(b)(2)(C).
222. Fed. R. Civ. P. 26(b)(1)(B).
223. Fed. R. Civ. P. 26(f).

privileges applicable to federal-law claims and defenses.[224] State law and federal law often recognize the same or similar privileges.

247. The attorney-client privilege is one of the oldest privileges for confidential communications. The privilege protects confidential communications between an attorney and the attorney's client related to the provision of legal advice. The privilege helps ensure full and frank communication between the attorney and the client, for purposes of facilitating the attorney-client relationship. It also avoids the awkward position of the attorney being made a witness against the client. The privilege can be waived if shared outside the zone of confidence. Sharing the information with non-attorney persons reasonably necessary to the attorney-client relationship, such as paralegals or interpreters, does not waive the privilege. The client holds the privilege and may prevent the attorney (or other involved party) from disclosing the information sought. Importantly, the *communication*, not the information, is privileged. Thus, a client cannot refuse to answer a question about what the client saw on the ground that the client has told the same information to their attorney. However, a client can refuse to answer a question about what the client told the attorney. Certain exceptions to the privilege exist, such as if the attorney is defending themselves against a legal-malpractice suit brought by the client, or if the communication is made in furtherance of a current or future crime or fraud.[225] A corporate client can engage in privileged communications with its attorney by communicating through corporate agents who direct the company or whose actions could bind the company.[226]

248. The federal courts have recognized other privileges. The clergy-communicant privilege "recognizes the human need to disclose to a spiritual counselor, in total and absolute confidence, what are believed to be flawed acts or thoughts and to receive priestly consolation and guidance in return."[227] The spousal privilege protects confidential oral communication between spouses. The doctor-patient privilege protects communications and records pertaining to health-related treatment. These privileges generally can be waived by the holder of the privilege.

249. The Federal Rules also protect from discovery certain information called "work product." Work product includes any materials prepared or formed by a party or representative in anticipation of litigation or for trial.[228] The idea is that each party can zealously pursue its case best when granted a confidential space for case development and strategy. Otherwise, each side would merely wait until the other side performed legal research or factual analysis and then request the other side's work in discovery.[229] Work-product protection may be lifted upon a showing of substantial need for the materials and undue hardship in acquiring them through other means, but if the court orders production, it must protect against the disclosure of

224. Fed. R. Evid. 501.
225. *In re Impounded Case (Law Firm)*, 879 F.2d 1211 (3rd Cir. 1989).
226. *Upjohn Co. v. United States*, 449 U.S. 383 (1981).
227. *In re Grand Jury Investigation*, 918 F.2d 374, 382 (3rd Cir. 1990).
228. Fed. R. Civ. P. 26(b)(3)(A).
229. *Hickman v. Taylor*, 329 U.S. 495 (1947).

so-called core work product—any mental impressions, conclusions, opinions, or legal theories of the party or representative.[230] The experts hired by a party fall within the scope of work product, but an expert who is designed as a testifying expert must waive the protection because the opponent is entitled to learn the basis for the expert's opinions.

§3. METHODS OF DISCOVERY

I. Initial Disclosures

250. The Federal Rules require the exchange of certain preliminary information deemed essential to all cases without awaiting a request for it: the name and contact information of persons likely to have discoverable information, along with the subject of that information, that the disclosing party may use to support its case; a copy or description of all documents in the disclosing party's possession that the disclosing party may use to support its case; a computation of damages claimed by the disclosing party; and a copy of any liability insurance policy that may apply to the disclosing party's liability in the case.[231] This information must be disclosed to the opposing party within fourteen days after the parties' initial discovery conference.

II. Depositions

251. Depositions are oral testimony taken under oath.[232] A party can take another party's deposition by providing a simple written advance notice. Nonparty depositions are generally obtained under subpoena.[233] Each party may take up to ten depositions unless modified by stipulation or court order. The deposition consists of a live question-and-answer session between the witness (the deponent) and the lawyer of the party who noticed the deposition. The deposition is conducted under oath, as would be trial testimony and is recorded by a court reporter. The deponent must answer based on personal knowledge. If disputes about the propriety of questions arise during a deposition, they may be objected to on the record, but the deponent generally must answer any question that does not call for privileged information, subject to any later exclusion by the court upon the recorded objection. As a matter of strategy, depositions occasionally serve to obtain testimony damaging to an opponent's case, but more often, they are used to learn all information within the knowledge of the deponent so that the parties will not be surprised by the deponent's testimony at trial. In rare cases, a deposition will be taken on written questions.[234]

---

230. Fed. R. Civ. P. 26(b)(3)(B).
231. Fed. R. Civ. P. 26(a)(1).
232. Fed. R. Civ. P. 30.
233. Fed. R. Civ. P. 45(d).
234. Fed. R. Civ. P. 31.

252. A party may depose a corporation or other business entity. In such a deposition notice, the party must describe with reasonable particularity the matters for examination. The business entity must then designate one or more representatives who can speak for the entity on the matters specified. Those representatives will then be deposed. They answer not in a personal capacity but rather on behalf of the entity.[235]

III. Interrogatories

253. Interrogatories consist of sets of written questions propounded by a party to another party in the litigation.[236] Unless otherwise stipulated or ordered by the court, interrogatories are limited to twenty-five questions, including subparts. Unlike depositions, interrogatories may be served only on other parties and not upon nonparty witnesses. Interrogatories are answered under oath, but they are questions posed to the party rather than an individual, so the responses must be based on party information rather than just personal information. A responding party thus has a duty to make reasonable efforts to ascertain the information requested. If the interrogatory asks for information contained in a document, the responding party can produce the document instead of answering.

IV. Requests for Production

254. A party can serve a request on another party or a subpoena on a nonparty for documents or other tangible things.[237] The request must describe the documents or categories of documents sought with reasonable particularity. Documents include intangible or electronic documents such as computer files, emails, texts, and voicemail recordings. Document discovery often involves monumental time, effort, and cost to search for, copy, review, and produce all documents responsive to a typical document request. At the same time, documentary evidence can be enormously useful, even crucial, to a party's case. Accordingly, document discovery is subject to intense negotiation between the parties to balance the needs of disclosure against the costs of production.

V. Requests for Admission

255. A party can serve a request on another party to admit specified factual averments.[238] The responding party must admit, deny, or assert insufficient information to be able to admit or deny. Generally, requests for admission do not obtain critical

235. Fed. R. Civ. P. 30(b)(6).
236. Fed. R. Civ. P. 33.
237. Fed. R. Civ. P. 34.
238. Fed. R. Civ. P. 34.

admissions that make or break a party's case. Instead, requests for admission usually help to isolate factual matters that, after the opportunity for other discovery, are no longer disputed. In addition, requests for admission can obtain technical admissions that streamline trial, such as obtaining admissions about the authenticity of a document, which otherwise would have to be proved at trial in order for the document to be admitted into evidence.

VI. Physical and Mental Examinations

256. The court may, for good cause, order a party whose physical or mental condition is in controversy to submit to an examination of that condition by a licensed professional. The examiner's findings and conclusions must be recorded in a written report.[239]

VII. International Discovery

257. When discoverable information is abroad, issues of international comity and judicial sovereignty are of central importance. Many countries object to the broad scope of U.S. discovery. Accordingly, discovery efforts in another country often must comply with foreign laws. However, discovery under the Federal Rules is proper if the discovery or deponent is in the United States, even if international issues are implicated. The Hague Evidence Convention provides additional methods for obtaining evidence in signatory countries.[240]

258. A federal statute allows litigants in a foreign proceeding to seek to obtain discovery in the United States.[241] The Supreme Court has given the statute broad reach.[242]

§4. Sanctions

259. When the parties cannot resolve a discovery dispute, one party will ask the judge to decide by filing a motion to compel or a motion for a protective order. When the judge decides the motion, the judge must order the losing party to pay the prevailing party's motion costs and fees unless the losing party's position was substantially justified.[243]

260. The violation of any discovery court order can be sanctioned by the judge through a variety of methods, including directing that the facts within the withheld

239. Fed. R. Civ. P. 35.
240. 28 U.S.C. §1781 note (Convention on the Taking of Evidence Abroad in Civil or Commercial Matters, 18 Mar. 1970, Ch. 1, Art. 1, 23 U.S.T. 2555, T.I.A.S. No. 7444).
241. 28 U.S.C. §1782(a).
242. *Intel Corp. v. Advanced Micro Devices*, 542 U.S. 241 (2004).
243. Fed. R. Civ. P. 37(a).

discovery be established as claimed by the prevailing party; striking pleadings, claims, or defenses; entering a default judgment; treating the violation as contempt of court; or imposing fines or cost or fee shifting.[244]

261. In addition, the attorney must sign all discovery requests and responses, and the attorney's signature is deemed to be a vertification that the discovery position is consistent with or warranted by a reasonable argument for modifying existing law, not imposed for any improper purpose such as delay or the imposition of cost, and is neither unreasonable nor unduly burdensome.[245] If a judge finds that an attorney has violated this verification, the court must impose an appropriate sanction, which may include attorney-fee shifting.[246]

244. Fed. R. Civ. P. 37(b).
245. Fed. R. Civ. P. 26(g)(1).
246. Fed. R. Civ. P. 26(g)(3).

Chapter 5. Summary Adjudication

§1. Dismissal

262. Claimants may dismiss their claims in several ways. A plaintiff may voluntarily dismiss an action unilaterally and without a court order simply by filing a notice of dismissal before the opposing party files either an answer or motion for summary judgment.[247] The rationale for this rule is that the plaintiff may have realized a mistake in filing in the wrong court or suing the wrong defendant or just determining that the burdens of litigation are too high in light of the expected reward. If the plaintiff wishes to get out of the lawsuit at a very early stage before the defendant has expended significant cost, the system will oblige.

263. The plaintiff also can voluntarily dismiss the action at any time by stipulation with the consent of all other parties.[248] The primary basis for this kind of dismissal is settlement. A settlement is a contract in which the defendant agrees to give the plaintiff some relief while the plaintiff agrees to dismiss the lawsuit. In nonclass cases, the court generally does not see, review, or approve of the settlement.

264. For either dismissal by notice or stipulation, the dismissal order is, by default, without prejudice unless the plaintiff previously dismissed any action based on the same claim. The default can be overridden by designation in the dismissal notice or stipulation.[249] Because dismissal stipulations are usually the result of a settlement, stipulations usually provide that the dismissal will be with prejudice, meaning the plaintiff will be barred from refiling the lawsuit.

265. If the plaintiff is not eligible to voluntarily dismiss the action by notice or stipulation, the plaintiff can file a motion for voluntary dismissal with the court. The court may grant the motion on terms that the court considers proper, including with cost or fee shifting against the plaintiff.[250] By default, the dismissal is without prejudice, but the order can override that default by specifying otherwise.

266. A court can order dismissal of claims asserted by a plaintiff who fails to pursue the case or comply with the rules or orders. This type of involuntary dismissal order is, by default, with prejudice unless the order specifies otherwise.[251]

267. Because of the need to protect absent class members, a certified class action may not be dismissed without the court's approval.[252]

247. Fed. R. Civ. P. 41(a)(1).
248. Fed. R. Civ. P. 41(a)(1).
249. Fed. R. Civ. P. 41(a)(1).
250. Fed. R. Civ. P. 41(a)(2).
251. Fed. R. Civ. P. 41(b).
252. Fed. R. Civ. P. 23(e).

§2. DEFAULT

268. Default is the flip side of dismissal but for defendants. The clerk of the court will enter a default against a defendant who fails to appear after proper service or who fails to defend after appearing.[253]

269. Upon entry of a default, the clerk can issue a default judgment if the complaint seeks a certain sum. If the complaint is not for a certain sum, the court must provide notice of a hearing to determine the appropriate damages.[254]

270. Two rationales animate the default rule. The first is to protect a defendant who does not wish to fight, such as if the defendant would admit all the plaintiff's allegations, if the defendant is judgment-proof, or if the defendant is confident that the court lacks jurisdiction. Such a defendant need not spend any money, time, or effort but rather may simply suffer a default judgment. The second rationale is to provide for an end to the litigation when one party refuses to litigate. The case must have an end, and, in those circumstances, the proper end is a default against that party.

271. Those rationales make sense in the circumstances they assume. Often, however, a default is entered despite the defendant's wish to defend. Service of process may, for example, not actually reach the defendant. In such circumstances, the default can be set aside for good cause, and a default judgment can be reopened under the reasons specified in the rule for reopening judgments.[255]

§3. RULE 68

272. To encourage joint party resolution, Rule 68 of the Federal Rules allows a defendant, at least fourteen days prior to trial, to serve an offer of judgment on the plaintiff, under specified terms and with costs then accrued. If the plaintiff formally accepts the offer, the clerk immediately enters judgment as specified by the parties, and the case closes. If the plaintiff rejects the offer, then the case continues, but the offer cannot be used as evidence. Further, if the plaintiff rejects the offer and then prevails on the merits but is awarded less than what was offered, then the plaintiff must pay the defendant's litigation costs incurred after the offer was made.[256]

273. Although they memorialize terms crafted and agreed upon by the parties, Rule 68 judgments differ from settlements in that Rule 68 offers and judgments are public documents, and the judgment has the imprimatur of a court order. By contrast, settlements usually are not public, not filed with the court, and have no judgment force.

253. Fed. R. Civ. P. 54(a).
254. Fed. R. Civ. P. 54(b).
255. Fed. R. Civ. P. 54(c).
256. Fed. R. Civ. P. 68.

§4. Summary Judgment

274. The close of discovery presents a major opportunity to end the case shy of trial: summary judgment. Although summary judgment can be entered at almost any time after the complaint and before trial, a summary judgment is based on evidence, and so, normally, summary judgment occurs after discovery. The evidentiary basis for a summary judgment distinguishes it from a dismissal.

275. The Seventh Amendment preserves a right to a trial by jury on factual disputes to which the jury-trial right attaches. Summary judgment is entered by the judge. To ensure that summary judgment does not infringe the right to a trial by jury, the standard for summary judgment is very high—essentially, the standard is that the evidence reveals that there is *not* a genuine dispute for trial. In other words, if all rational juries would reach the same conclusion about a factual dispute, then it is not a genuine dispute, and the judge can resolve it without submitting it to the jury.[257] Importantly, the judge does not weigh the evidence or assess credibility. Rather, the judge must predict whether a rational jury could, viewing all the evidence in the light most favorable to the nonmovant, find for the nonmovant.

276. A party can move for summary judgment by identifying the claim, defense, or issue on which summary judgment is sought and pointing to admissible evidence in the discovery record, showing that no rational jury could find for the nonmovant. If the party is correct, then the nonmovant can avoid summary judgment either by augmenting the record with additional admissible evidence that would create a genuine dispute for trial or by showing that the nonmovant has not yet had full opportunity to complete discovery on the issue.[258]

277. In practice, summary judgment generally takes two forms. An "affirmative evidence" motion marshalls the evidence in favor of the movant that tends to disprove or refute an essential element of the opponent's case. This type of summary judgment is very difficult to obtain because of the difficulty of excluding the possibility that a rational jury might discredit that evidence in favor of the evidence supporting the nonmovant.[259] A "no evidence" motion is always filed by the party without the burden of proof at trial and argues that the record contains no evidence to support an essential element of the nonmovant's case. The idea is that a party who must prove a fact by a preponderance of the evidence mathematically cannot do so if the party has no evidence on that issue because zero can never be a preponderance.[260]

278. Summary judgment has rightly been criticized as enabling judges to substitute their own judgment for that of a rational jury. Judges see many cases, and they often think they know what a jury will do, but the proper standard is not what

257. Fed. R. Civ. P. 56(a).
258. Fed. R. Civ. P. 56(c).
259. E.g., *Adickes v. S. H. Kress & Co.*, 398 U.S. 144 (1970).
260. E.g., *Celotex Corp. v. Catrett*, 477 U.S. 317 (1986).

a particular jury is likely to do but whether *all* juries will fine for the nonmovant. That difficulty is highlighted by a case called *Scott v. Harris*,[261] in which a police officer rammed the back of a suspect's car during a high-speed chase. The suspect was injured and sued the officer for excessive force. The substantive law immunized the officer if the conduct was "reasonable" under the circumstances, a question of fact for the jury. The officer moved for summary judgment and pointed to police car dash cameras of the chase and its conclusion. The Supreme Court, in an 8-1 decision, upheld summary judgment for the officer. The Court found the tape so compelling that, in its view, all juries would find the officer's conduct to be reasonable. However, in a compelling study conducted after the decision, researchers showed the video to hundreds of prospective jurors and reached a different conclusion. The data showed that although a majority of viewers believed the officer's conduct to be reasonable, a substantial minority did not. Further, the researchers showed that viewer's conclusions varied based on cultural, ideological, and other attributes.[262] The study suggests that a rational jury could, indeed, have found the officer's conduct to be unreasonable.

261. 550 U.S. 372 (2007).

262. Dan M. Kahan, David A. Hoffman & Donald Braman, *Whose Eyes Are You Going to Believe? Scott v. Harris and the Perils of Cognitive Illiberalism*, 122 Harv. L. Rev. 837 (2009).

Chapter 6. Trial

279. If a claim survives summary judgment, then the case proceeds to trial. The judge will hold a final pretrial conference in which each party identifies the documents it intends to introduce, the witnesses it intends to call, and the time it plans to take on each witness.[263] The parties may even litigate the admissibility of some of the evidence at that time through motions *in limine*. This final exchange of information is not exactly a script of the trial, but it is designed to reduce—if not eliminate—any surprises. Civil trials are not like the usual courtroom dramas of Hollywood fame. What comes out at trial may be new and surprising to the jury, but it is rarely new or surprising to the lawyers and litigants.

280. Trial can be either a bench trial or a jury trial. This Chapter addresses both types. It then summarizes some of the principal issues of the presentation and admission of evidence.

§1. Bench Trial

281. A bench trial occurs before a judge, who acts as both trier of fact and decider of law. Bench trials proceed for any claim to which the Seventh Amendment right does not attach and to any claim for which the parties have waived their jury-trial rights. At the conclusion of the presentation of evidence, the judge will make written findings of fact and conclusions of law in justifying the verdict.[264]

§2. Jury Trial

I. Jury Right

282. The Seventh Amendment provides that the parties have a right to a jury in suits at common law for more than USD 20, and no fact tried by a jury shall be reexamined except according to the rules of the common law.[265] The Seventh Amendment applies only in federal court,[266] though most states have parallel constitutional provisions providing for jury trials in state courts. At the time of the Founding, the jury was seen as a crucial bulwark against the perceived tyranny and bias of judges who might have harbored sympathies with the Crown.

283. The Seventh Amendment only applies to suits at common law, but American law has largely merged law and equity today. Further, the common law is distinct from statutory law, but many statutes purport to codify or augment the common law. In *Dimick v. Schiedt*, the Supreme Court clarified that the Seventh Amendment

263. Fed. R. Civ. P. 16(e).
264. Fed. R. Civ. P. 52(a).
265. U.S. Const. Amend. VII.
266. *Minneapolis v. St. Louis Railroad Co. v. Bombolis*, 241 U.S. 211 (1916).

applies to cases that would have fallen under the common law of England in 1791, when the Amendment was adopted.[267] Further, when legal issues are joined with equitable issues, the Seventh Amendment requires that the legal issues be determined by a jury first.[268] In a mixed case, the parties can consent to a jury trial of equitable issues, even though a jury would not be constitutionally required.[269]

284. When the Seventh Amendment guarantees a jury-trial right, the parties must preserve that right by demanding it in a timely fashion. A demand must be served on the opposing party within fourteen days after the last pleading directed to the issue is served.[270] Often, the plaintiff will demand trial by jury on all such triable issues in the complaint, and the defendant will do the same in the answer. However, preservation of the right is subject to subsequent withdrawal of the demand upon the consent of all parties.[271] Not uncommonly, parties will timely demand a jury trial but later withdraw the demand and stipulate to a bench trial, which may be able to be scheduled more conveniently and which they expect to be of shorter duration than a jury trial.

II. Jury Selection

285. The clerk of the court calls a *venire*, or jury pool, from a randomized call of the eligible residents within the geographic region of the court. Some residents called may, for good cause, receive excuses or postponements from the clerk in advance. They may be called again. The rest arrive at court, fill out a form with basic demographic, educational, and professional information, and then proceed to the assigned courtroom.

286. The venire inside the courtroom can number between fifty and one hundred persons. From this number, the court will select between six and twelve as the jury. Most federal courts try to empanel a jury of ten to twelve, sometimes with additional alternates. The process of winnowing down the venire to a jury is called *voir dire*, or, in common parlance, jury selection.

287. Jury selection entails two stages. The first stage is the examination. Federal practice tends toward examination by the judge rather than by the lawyers, but individual examination by the lawyers is sometimes permitted after the judge has finished.[272] The questions are designed to determine if any person has some bias or prejudice In the case that might inhibit their ability to be impartial or to fairly consider all the evidence. For example, in an employment discrimination case, a person whose spouse was just terminated, unfairly in the person's view, might not be able to judge the evidence of the case fairly. Or perhaps the venireperson has a longtime

267. 293 U.S. 474 (1935).
268. *Beacon Theaters v. Westover*, 359 U.S. 500 (1959), *Dairy Queen v. Wood*, 369 U.S. 469 (1962).
269. Fed. R. Civ. P. 39(c).
270. Fed. R. Civ. P. 38(b).
271. Fed. R. Civ. P. 38(d).
272. Fed. R. Civ. P. 47(a).

personal friendship with the defendant's counsel. The questions are also designed to elicit any health or personal circumstances that might make jury service uncomfortable or unfair for the juror. For example, someone undergoing intense chemotherapy treatment may not be able to serve effectively as a juror in a two-week case. Finally, the questions are designed to give the attorneys a sense of how the juror might view the parties' cases.

288. During and after questioning, the judge will excuse some members of the venire for good cause, meaning the person is not fit to serve as a juror in the case, either for reasons of partiality or inability to serve.[273] In the federal system and most states, each party is also given the chance to make a number of so-called peremptory strikes.[274] These are opportunities for parties to remove jurors without demonstrating good cause. These peremptory strikes, or challenges, can be used for any reason or no reason at all, except that they cannot be based on the race or gender of the juror.[275] Once the cause and peremptory removals are completed, the jury is seated from among the remaining first-numbered venirepersons, and then the rest are excused from service.

III. Jury Role

289. Even during a jury trial, the decision-making responsibilities are divided between the jury and the judge. Generally, the jury decides matters of fact and the judge decides matters of law. Whether the defendant breached a contract, then, is generally a question of fact for the jury, while the admissibility of evidence is a question of law for the judge. However, some factual issues may be decided by a judge. In *Markman v. Westview Instruments, Inc.*,[276] the Supreme Court held that, in a jury trial for patent infringement, the judge should determine the meaning and scope of the patent, while the jury should determine whether the patent has been infringed. The Court first looked to historical approaches but found no appropriate analogous approach taken by common-law courts at the time of the Seventh Amendment. Instead, the Court reasoned that functional reasons supported the conclusion that judges should construe patents because they are more familiar with the technical legalese of patent language and because they can provide a uniform construction of a patent that will settle the patent's meaning to stave off future disputes.

IV. Jury Deliberation and Verdict

290. At the close of the presentation of the evidence, the judge will instruct the jury on the matters for jury deliberation and decision, including providing the jury with guidance about the standards to be used. For example, the judge will often

273. Fed. R. Civ. P. 47(c).
274. Fed. R. Civ. P. 47(b).
275. *J.E.B. v. Alabama*, 511 U.S. 127 (1994); *Edmonson v. Leesville Concrete Co.*, 500 U.S. 614 (1991).
276. 517 U.S. 370 (1996).

explain the burden of proof, the role of defenses, and the differences between various kinds of damages. What instructions are given are matters of law that, if made in error, are appealable issues, so the judge will often ask the parties to draft the instructions jointly, with an eye toward using language that the parties can agree upon, though the judge must ultimately decide what instructions to give. Vetted and published model jury instructions are available to aid this process.

291. Upon receiving the instructions, the jury will retire to the deliberation room to discuss the case in secret. The deliberations are not recorded.

292. In federal court, the jury must decide issues unanimously unless the parties have stipulated otherwise.[277] Some states allow verdicts based on less than unanimity.[278] During deliberations, the jury will complete a verdict form. The verdict form can either be a general verdict, which simply announces who wins and, if the plaintiff, for how much, though the judge also can include questions requiring specific findings of fact; or a special verdict, which requires the jury to answer a series of findings that then lead to the conclusion of who wins and for how much.[279] If the jury cannot reach a unanimous verdict, the judge will declare a mistrial and set a date for a new trial with a different jury selected from a new venire.

277. Fed. R. Civ. P. 48(b).
278. E.g., Cal. Const. Art. I, §6.
279. Fed. R. Civ. P. 49.

Chapter 7. Post-Trial Motions and Judgment

§1. Judgment as a Matter of Law

293. At the conclusion of the plaintiff's presentation of her case-in-chief at trial, the defense can and typically does move for a judgment as a matter of law (sometimes called a directed verdict), arguing that the evidence presented by plaintiff is not sufficient to enable a finder of fact, acting rationally, to find in the plaintiff's favor on at least one required element of the plaintiff's claim.[280] The standard is analytically identical to the summary-judgment standard described earlier, except that a summary judgment is based on the admissible evidence in the discovery record, while a judgment as a matter of law is based on the evidence actually admitted into evidence at trial so far. In both cases, the judge cannot decide the motion based on the judge's own view of the evidence but rather must predict whether a rational jury, viewing the evidence in the light most favorable to the nonmovant, could find the nonmovant.

294. At the conclusion of the defendant's case and the rebuttal presentations, one or both sides may move for a directed verdict, once again arguing that a rational trier of fact could come out only one way in the case. If no motion is granted, then the parties make their closing arguments and then the case is submitted to the fact-finder for a verdict.

295. Upon the rendering of a verdict, the losing party then may, if the party previously made a pre-verdict motion for judgment as a matter of law, renew that motion post-verdict (sometimes called a JNOV or judgment notwithstanding the verdict).[281] The standard remains the same but now requires a finding that the verdict is irrational (or that some legal conclusion requires the entry of judgment for the losing party). A post-jury-verdict judgment as a matter of law does not violate the Seventh Amendment's prohibition on reexamination of jury findings because the post-verdict motion is not a new motion but rather a renewal of a pre-verdict motion.

§2. New Trial

296. Another post-verdict motion with a lower standard than a judgment as a matter of law is a motion for a new trial.[282] The grounds for a new trial may include evidentiary rulings that a judge made during trial that erroneously admitted or excluded material evidence that may have made a difference in the outcome, the discovery of new evidence, juror misconduct, or simply that the verdict is "against the weight of the evidence." Unlike on a motion for a judgment as a matter of law, the judge may grant a new trial upon simply disagreeing with the result, based on the

280. Fed. R. Civ. P. 50(a).
281. Fed. R. Civ. P. 50(b).
282. Fed. R. Civ. P. 59.

judge's own assessment of the evidence. However, because a new trial calls into question the unanimous view of the jury and entails significant cost and delay for the parties to retry the case, judges often exercise their discretion to order new trials very sparingly.

297. Sometimes, judges will use their power to grant new trials to get the parties to agree to modify the jury verdict to something the judge thinks is more fair. For example, a judge may give a prevailing plaintiff an option: accept less money than the jury awarded or endure the expense and uncertainty of an entirely new trial. Such a device is known as "remittitur," and has been held not to violate a party's constitutional right to a jury trial.

§3. Judgment and Costs

298. The entry of a judgment is the judicial act that gives effect to a jury verdict or court decision. The formal entry of a judgment is a significant event because it establishes the time of judgment, which begins the running of rigid deadlines for post-trial motions and appeals. The entry of a judgment also signifies the final determination of an action.[283]

299. Although the American Rule is that each party bears its own costs and fees of litigation, the rules direct that the prevailing party is entitled to reimbursement of litigation costs from the losing party unless federal law or a court order directs otherwise.[284] Attorney's fees generally shift only when specifically provided by statute or court order.[285]

§4. Preclusion

I. Introduction

300. Preclusion law in the United States governs the preclusive effect given to prior litigation in subsequent litigation. The law of preclusion is often usefully divided into two subcategories: claim preclusion (also known as res judicata) and issue preclusion (also known as collateral estoppel).

II. Claim Preclusion

301. The general rule of claim preclusion is as follows: a valid, final judgment, rendered on the merits, constitutes a bar to a subsequent action between the same parties, or those in privity with them, for the same dispute.[286]

283. Fed. R. Civ. P. 54(c).
284. Fed. R. Civ. P. 54(d)(1).
285. Fed. R. Civ. P. 54(d)(2).
286. *Taylor v. Sturgell*, 553 U.S. 880 (2008).

302. Claim preclusion binds the parties both as to claims and defenses actually litigated and determined in the first suit and as to related claims and defenses that were not raised in the first action. Relatedness is governed, in federal court and in most state courts, by the same-transaction-or-occurrence test. Under this test, a claim or defense pleaded in the second action is precluded if the facts which constitute it arose out of the same transaction or occurrence that served as the basis for the first litigation.

III. Issue Preclusion

303. The general rule of issue preclusion is as follows: A person is "estopped" or precluded from relitigating any issue of law or fact if the issue was actually litigated, was necessarily determined, and was essential to a valid and final judgment entered previously in litigation to which that person was a party, provided the estopped party had a full and fair opportunity and adequate incentive to litigate the issue conclusively, and subject to additional fairness constraints that arise when the party asserting the estoppel is not a party to the prior action.[287]

304. Some elements are common to both claim and issue preclusion. The rules for what counts as a valid and final judgment on the merits are largely the same for the two doctrines, as are the rules for determining the parties bound by the earlier action. The key difference is that while claim preclusion forecloses whole causes of action, issue preclusion prevents relitigation of discrete issues, whether or not those issues are central to the later litigation. Also, claim preclusion forecloses not only claims and defenses actually litigated but also related claims and defenses that were not, whereas issue preclusion forecloses only issues that were in fact litigated, fought over, and indeed necessary to the prior judgment. Finally, under certain circumstances, issue preclusion may be invoked by someone who was not a party to the earlier action; claim preclusion may be invoked only by a party involved in the first case.

305. A major development in the law of issue preclusion over the last fifty years has been the decline in the requirement of mutuality. At common law, issue preclusion could be invoked only by one who was a party to the first action. The theory was that if someone was not going to be bound by an adverse result in the first action (as non-parties would not be), then fairness required that this person not be able to benefit from the first action either. But recently, the U.S. Supreme Court has held that as long as a party to the first action had full and fair opportunity and incentive to litigate the issue, then that party can be held to issue preclusion, even by someone who had no stake in the earlier action.

287. *Parklane Hosiery Co. v. Shore*, 439 U.S. 322 (1979).

§5. RELIEF FROM JUDGMENT

306. The rules allow relief from judgment in certain contexts. If the judgment as issued contains a clerical mistake, such as a typographical error, the court can correct the judgment on its own or on motion of a party.[288]

307. Relief from judgment for other reasons requires a motion by a party. Other reasons include mistake, inadvertence, or excusable neglect; newly discovered evidence that could not have been discovered in time to move for a new trial; fraud, misrepresentation, or misconduct by the opposing party; the judgment is void; the judgment has been satisfied or cannot equitably continue to be applied; or any other reason that justifies relief.[289] Courts have construed the final catchall "any other reason" to require extraordinary circumstances.[290] A motion for relief from judgment for any of these reasons must be made within a reasonable time and, for the first three reasons, no later than one year after entry of judgment.[291]

§6. APPEAL

I. Who Can Appeal

308. In general, a party that does not receive all requested relief may appeal a trial-court judgment to an intermediate Court of Appeals. Usually, the losing party appeals, but the winning party can appeal if the winning party does not receive as much of a win as originally requested. Sometimes, both parties appeal.

II. Issues for Appeal

309. Generally, only issues properly raised and decided by the lower court can be the basis for appeal. This requirement encourages parties to present important issues to the trial court in the first instance. Most jurisdictions have exceptions to this requirement: for issues that were futile to raise before the trial court given its other rulings or issues that are so fundamental that fairness requires an appellate court to examine them, even if the appellant had no good reason for not having given the trial court a chance to consider the issue. There is also an exception for defects of subject-matter jurisdiction, which can be raised at any time on appeal, whether pressed by appellant below or not.

288. Fed. R. Civ. P. 60(a).
289. Fed. R. Civ. P. 60(b).
290. *Ackermann v. United States*, 340 U.S. 193 (1950).
291. Fed. R. Civ. P. 60(c)(1).

III. The Final Judgment Rule

310. In the federal system, appeals ordinarily lie only from "final decisions" of the district courts.[292] Most, but by no means all, of the state jurisdictions follow a similar approach. A final decision is one that "ends the litigation on the merits and leaves nothing to do but execute the judgment."[293] Thus, under the federal model, the ordinary rule—subject to a number of statutory exceptions—is that no appeal may be taken from errors in the course of trial and the pretrial process until the litigation in the trial court has run its entire course and a final judgment has been entered. Thus, for example, if a party wants to appeal a discovery ruling or a trial court evidentiary ruling, he must wait until the trial court proceedings are finished and then appeal if he was a losing party in the case. The final judgment rule tends to preserve appellate resources because some disputes—such as a dispute over discovery—will never be appealed if the party who lost on the disputed pretrial issue nonetheless wins the overall case at the trial level. But it may waste trial resources because an error that would have disposed of the case early cannot be appealed until the case concludes through other means, sometimes years of litigation later.

311. Several exceptions to the final judgment rule exist. Under the "collateral-order doctrine," immediate appeal is allowed for a small class of prejudgment orders that "finally determine claims of right separable from, and collateral to, rights asserted in the action [and that are] too important to be denied review and too independent of the cause itself to require that appellate consideration be deferred until the whole case is adjudicated."[294] To fall within this exception, an order must conclusively determine the question from which appeal is sought, the issue resolved must be important and completely separate from the merits of the action, and it must be effectively unreviewable on appeal from a final judgment.[295] An example is the denial of a motion to dismiss based on a defendant's assertion of official immunity.

312. Another important exception allows appeals from interlocutory orders (i.e., orders which are not final judgments) of the district court "granting, continuing, modifying, refusing or dissolving injunctions, or refusing to dissolve or modify injunctions."[296] This exception is based on the potentially irreparable harm that may be caused by an erroneous injunction or suffered if an injunction is erroneously denied.

313. Yet another important exception permits the district court to certify that a particular interlocutory order "involves a controlling question of law as to which there is substantial ground for difference of opinion" and that "an immediate appeal

292. 28 U.S.C. §1291.
293. *Catlin v. United States*, 324 U.S. 229, 233 (1945).
294. *Cohen v. Beneficial Industrial Loan Corp.*, 337 U.S. 541, 546 (1949).
295. *Gulfstream Aerospace Corp. v. Mayacamas Corp.*, 485 U.S. 271, 277 (1988).
296. 28 U.S.C. §1292(a).

from the order may materially advance the ultimate termination of the litigation."[297] The Court of Appeals then has discretionary power to grant or deny review of the certified question.

314. Finally, the decision of a motion for class certification is subject to interlocutory appeal.[298]

IV. The Mechanics of Appeal

315. In most American systems, one takes an appeal by filing a "notice of appeal," which tells the appellate court and the parties that a formal appeal is forthcoming. This notice must be made within a period of time specified by federal statute,[299] and the period of time is inflexible except as expressly provided in the statute.[300]

316. After notice of appeal is filed, the appellant must prepare and file the record, which is an excerpted version of the full official record of the trial court that covers the matters on which appeal will be taken. The parties then file briefs with their arguments regarding any reversible errors by the trial court. Oral argument is generally permitted, though the federal rules permit a Court of Appeals to order a case heard without oral argument.[301] When oral argument is heard, the appellate judges (in the federal system sitting as panels of three judges) not only hear the views of counsel for the parties but also ask counsel any questions the judges may have. The case is then submitted to the appellate court, and a decision is announced at a later date. The time between oral argument and decision varies greatly between courts and cases, from weeks to (rarely) years.

V. The Scope of Appellate Review

317. Even after an appellate court has taken a case, it will not disturb the ruling by the trial court unless it falls within the description of reversible error. Whether an error is reversible depends upon: (1) the standard of review applied by the appellate court, and (2) whether the error affected the result in the trial court.

318. An appellate court reviews errors of fact under a deferential "clearly erroneous" standard of review. This means that, as to findings of fact, an appellate court will not reverse even if it disagrees with the trial court's findings, unless the trial court's findings are *clearly* wrong. In other words, under this standard, an appellate court is not supposed to substitute its own factual findings for those of the trial court

297. 28 U.S.C. §1292(b).
298. Fed. R. Civ. P. 23(f).
299. 28 U.S.C. §2107.
300. *Bowles v. Russell*, 551 U.S. 205 (2007).
301. Fed. R. App. P. 34.

but only to ensure that the trial court's findings fall within a range of reasonable discretion about what findings to make. This standard, at least in the federal system, applies whether the trial court's findings of fact are based on documentary evidence or live testimony.[302]

319. An appellate court's review of the trial court's interpretations of law, by contrast, is "de novo" or "from the beginning." Under this standard, an appellate court will displace a trial court's legal rulings if the appellate court has come to a different ruling in the first instance, even if the trial court's rulings are not outside the range of reasonableness. Of course, even under this "de novo" standard, an appellate court will take into account the reasoning of the trial court and will give due respect to the experience and judgment of the trial judge.

320. Even if a Court of Appeals applying the appropriate standard of review concludes that the trial court has erred, it will affirm the trial court if the error would not have affected the result. In civil litigation, the so-called harmless error rule (by which harmless errors are ignored) requires a party seeking appellate reversal to show a substantial probability that, but for the error, the judgment would have been more favorable to the appellant. This rule is but another illustration that appellate courts will not lightly overturn judgments and that appellate courts are pragmatic in their focus on the result below rather than the reasoning of the lower court.

VI. Appealing from an Appellate Court

321. After a Court of Appeals has rendered its decision, usually acting through a three-judge panel, a dissatisfied party may ask the entire appellate court (from which the three-judge panel was drawn) to hear the case in full, or "en banc." Such en banc review is available at the discretion of a majority of the judges of the appellate court. En banc review usually will be denied unless the case is very important or involves a legal ruling that conflicts with that of other appellate courts. If en banc review is granted, the three-judge panel decision is vacated, new briefs are written, new oral arguments are had, and the whole Court of Appeals decides the case.

322. A party dissatisfied with the ruling of the Court of Appeals can seek review in the U.S. Supreme Court. Today, the Supreme Court's docket is almost entirely discretionary. The court's internal operating rules require that four of the nine justices on the court vote to hear a case before discretionary review (formally called a writ of certiorari) is granted. The Supreme Court does not sit primarily to correct mistakes of trial courts or courts of appeals. Instead, the court views its primary function as clarifying important and recurring questions of federal constitutional and statutory law. For that reason, the Court usually will hear only cases presenting issues over which the lower courts are split and cases that are otherwise of fundamental importance to the proper application of federal law.

302. Fed. R. Civ. P. 52(a).

Part IV. Evidence

Chapter 1. Overview

323. The plaintiff, or more specifically, the party with the burden of proof, generally makes the first opening statement and at the end of trial makes the last closing argument. The opening statement is a preview of the evidence of the case and a framework for organizing that evidence so that the finder of fact will understand how each piece of evidence introduced fits into the party's theory of the case. The defendant's lawyer usually follows by making an opening statement to present the defendant's view of the evidence and theory of the case.

324. The plaintiff then proceeds to present the "case-in-chief," which consists of the testimony of witnesses called by the plaintiff and examined by her lawyer, including the presentation of real and documentary evidence which the plaintiff believes supports the facts she must prove to establish liability under the applicable substantive law. During the case-in-chief, the defendant and other parties have the opportunity to object to the introduction of evidence and to have their lawyers cross-examine witnesses presented by the plaintiff.

Chapter 2. Presumptions and Burdens of Proof

325. The burden of proof can be described as the duty borne by a party ultimately to convince the trier of fact (the jury in a jury trial or the judge in a bench trial) that all the essential elements of the claim or defense are proved by the evidence presented. The burden of proof is sometimes also called the burden of persuasion. Under either terminology, a party who bears the burden but who fails to discharge it loses on the particular claim or defense at issue. Factors that influence which party has the burden of proof include policy considerations, such as the desire to encourage or discourage a particular type of litigation, and fairness considerations, such as which party has control over the evidence relevant to a fact or element.

326. Identifying who bears the *burden* of proof is to be distinguished from defining the *standard* of proof itself. In most civil cases in the United States, the standard of proof used is a preponderance of the evidence; that is, a party who bears the burden of proof must convince a finder of fact to conclude that a preponderance of the evidence weighs in the party's favor on the disputed fact or issue. The preponderance standard has, in turn, been defined to mean that a party who bears the burden must prove the disputed proposition asserted by that party is more likely true than not true. This preponderance standard is much less onerous than, for example, the standard used in most American criminal cases—the standard of "beyond a reasonable doubt." In some civil lawsuits, like fraud or defamation, or for certain remedies, like punitive damages, the common law has developed a standard of proof in between the preponderance and the reasonable-doubt standards: the "clear and convincing evidence" standard.[303]

303. E.g., *Colorado v. New Mexico*, 467 U.S. 310 (1984).

Chapter 3. Rules of Evidence

327. The Federal Rules of Evidence (FRE) govern the presentation and admission of evidence in both bench and jury trials.

§1. Relevance Versus Prejudice

328. Only evidence logically relevant to a claim or defense is admissible.[304] The concept of logical relevance is itself defined as evidence tending to make the existence of any material fact more probable or less probable than it would be without the evidence.[305] Material facts comprise the elements of a claim or defense. They can be direct evidence of the elements, inferences and circumstantial evidence of the elements, or facts that bear upon the credibility of other evidence. All logically relevant evidence is admissible except as provided by federal law.

329. Evidence is inadmissible, despite being logically related, if the probative value is substantially outweighed by the danger of unfair prejudice, confusion of the issues, misleading of the jury, undue delay, waste of time, or needless presentation of cumulative evidence.[306]

§2. General Types of Evidence

330. Evidence used in judicial proceedings falls into three categories: direct evidence, circumstantial evidence, and real evidence. "Direct evidence" is eyewitness testimony and other testimony that goes directly to the proposition to be established. "Circumstantial evidence" is evidence of circumstances that requires the finder of fact to draw an inference. Circumstantial evidence is not inherently less persuasive or less reliable than direct evidence. It simply requires the finder of fact to take the extra step of making an inference. "Real evidence," when presented, permits the trier of fact to make his own determination. Real evidence is based on the juror's or judge's own perceptions, often using senses other than sight in making the determination. For example, a sample of intoxicating liquor may be given to the jury, from which they will decide, based on their own observations, if it is actually intoxicating liquor. Other examples of real evidence include photographs, bodily demonstrations, audio-video evidence, models, maps, and the like.

304. Fed. R. Evid. 402.
305. Fed. R. Evid. 401.
306. Fed. R. Evid. 403.

§3. Specific Types of Evidence

I. Character Evidence

331. Generally, character evidence cannot be used to prove action in conformity therewith on a particular occasion.[307] However, if the character of the party is a genuine issue in the case, evidence of that character may be admitted. Further, character evidence may be admissible for other purposes, including motive, opportunity, intent, preparation, absence of mistake or accident, knowledge, and identity. In addition, evidence of character, which is generally inadmissible to prove conforming conduct, is different from evidence of habit, which generally is admissible to prove conforming conduct.[308] Finally, character evidence may be used to impeach a witness's testimony. In all cases, the character evidence that is unfairly prejudicial is always subject to the general rule of exclusion.

II. Subsequent Remedial Measures

332. Evidence of changes or repairs made after the event in question has occurred is not admissible to prove negligence or culpable conduct in connection with the event. The evidence may be offered for other purposes, including proving ownership, control, or feasibility of precautionary measures, or impeachment, if any of these facts is disputed.[309] The policy behind this rule is straightforward: society does not want to do anything that discourages parties from making repairs or changes after an accident. The rule also reflects the belief that a change in design after an accident does not necessarily mean that the original design was defective and that not all triers of fact will be analytically careful in this regard.

III. Offers of Compromise

333. Evidence of offers to compromise or settle a claim is inadmissible to prove liability for or invalidity of the claim or its amount. Evidence of conduct or statements made in compromise negotiations are also inadmissible.[310] Settlement evidence may be admissible for purposes other than liability, such as to prove bias or prejudice or to contest a contention of undue delay.

IV. Liability Insurance

334. Evidence that a defendant has procured liability insurance is inadmissible to prove liability.[311] The evidence may be admissible if offered for another purpose,

307. Fed. R. Evid. 404.
308. Fed. R. Evid. 406.
309. Fed. R. Evid. 407.
310. Fed. R. Evid. 408.
311. Fed. R. Evid. 411.

such as proof of agency ownership or control (when in dispute) or to impeach a witness. The evidence may also be admitted where admission of liability comes by implication from a reference to the fact or effect of insurance, as when an alleged tortfeasor tells the injured party: "Don't worry. My insurance company will take care of everything."

§4. Authentication and Best Evidence

335. Authentication that the proffered evidence is what it purports to be is a prerequisite of admission.[312] Authentication is usually provided through oral testimony of a witness familiar with the document or other piece of evidence proffered for admission. Questions such as "Did you take this photograph? What does the photograph depict?" or "Can you identify this document? What is it?" are common ways to authenticate a document. Some types of evidence—public documents under seal or bearing an authorized signature, foreign public documents, certified copies of public records, newspapers and periodicals, official publications, and documents accompanied by a certificate of acknowledgment—are self-authenticating.[313] The parties can, and often do, stipulate in advance the authenticity of evidence likely to be proffered at trial so that the presentation of proof is not disrupted by continual authentication.

336. The best evidence rule is the name given to the law's preference for the production of an original of a writing, recording, or photograph, where the contents of the item are material.[314] The rule was developed at common law to prevent inaccuracy and fraud. In practice, however, parties commonly stipulate to the admissibility of reliable copies of original documents.

§5. Hearsay

I. The Hearsay Rule

337. "Hearsay" is defined as an out-of-court statement offered to prove the truth of the matter asserted in the statement.[315] Hearsay need not be an oral statement. Written assertions and nonverbal assertive conduct may also be considered hearsay. In most cases, evidence that meets the hearsay definition will be excluded from the proceeding.

338. Hearsay exclusion has three justifications. First, live witnesses are required to take the oath, whereas out-of-court declarants are (in most cases) not under oath when they make their statement. Second, if the declarant gives testimony in front of

312. Fed. R. Evid. 901.
313. Fed. R. Evid. 902.
314. Fed. R. Evid. 1001.
315. Fed. R. Evid. 801.

the finder of fact, the finder of fact can evaluate the demeanor of the witness and use its observations to aid in measuring credibility. Finally, out-of-court declarants are not subject to cross-examination. During cross-examination, the witness may be probed concerning veracity, the accuracy of initial perceptions, and quality of memory.

339. Hearsay is only excluded if proffered as evidence of the truth of the matter asserted. By contrast, hearsay offered to show that certain words were spoken—i.e., that the statement was, in fact, made, irrespective of its veracity—will not be excluded. Hearsay is admissible if used to establish, for example, the declarant's mental state at the time in question or where the mere speaking of words is a fact in itself that has legal operation, such as words that constitute an oral contract.

II. Hearsay Exemptions

340. Even when hearsay testimony is proffered for the truth of the matter asserted, the rules exempt certain admissions of a party opponent, prior guilty pleas, judicial admissions, and vicarious admissions and statements of coconspirators.[316] Hearsay statements falling within these exemptions are not hearsay and therefore admissible if relevant and not unduly prejudicial.

III. Hearsay Exceptions

341. Some statements, though within the definition of inadmissible hearsay, nevertheless fall within designated exceptions to the hearsay rule.

A. *Unavailability Exceptions*

342. Certain classes of hearsay statements by the declarant are deemed to be made under conditions of reliability and will fall within an exception to the hearsay rule if the declarant is unavailable to be a witness at trial.[317] Qualifying unavailability reasons include death, physical or mental illness, refusal to testify, lack of memory concerning the incident, or witnesses who have been exempted from testifying on the ground of privilege, are beyond the subpoena power of the court, or are missing.

1. Declarations against Interest

343. Hearsay statements that are against a declarant's pecuniary, proprietary, or penal interest are admissible against the declarant.[318] In order for a statement against

316. Fed. R. Evid. 801(d).
317. Fed. R. Evid. 804(a).
318. Fed. R. Evid. 804(b)(3).

the declarant's penal interest to be admissible, corroborating circumstances must clearly indicate the trustworthiness of the statement.[319]

2. Dying Declarations

344. Declarations by a person who is dying are an exception to the hearsay rule if the declarant believed that death was imminent at the time of the statement.[320] Most courts also require that the declarant actually died as a result of the incident.

B. Other Exceptions

345. Other hearsay exceptions involve statements that, in light of the surrounding circumstances, are presumed to be reliable. The declarant need not be unavailable.

1. Excited Utterances

346. A statement relating to a startling event or condition made while the declarant was under the stress of excitement caused by the event or condition is an exception to the hearsay rule.[321] Some courts also require that the statement be spontaneous and not made in response to questions. Courts believe that the circumstances surrounding the statement lend special reliability because the declarant generally does not have enough time between the event and the statement to fabricate the content of the statement. In addition, the declarant's perception of the event is likely to be more accurate at the time than later in court, such that the excited utterance is actually more reliable than the live testimony.

2. Present-Sense Impression

347. For similar reasons, a declaration of a present-sense impression that describes the event at issue and is made almost simultaneously with the event described falls under a hearsay exception.[322] Extending the exception to a statement of recent perception was rejected by Congress.

3. Statements of Present Physical Condition or State of Mind

348. Statements of the declarant's existing state of mind, emotion, sensation, or physical condition are also an exception to the hearsay rule.[323] The rationale is that

319. *Williamson v. United States*, 512 U.S. 594 (1994).
320. Fed. R. Evid. 804(b)(2).
321. Fed. R. Evid. 803(2).
322. Fed. R. Evid. 803(1).
323. Fed. R. Evid. 803(3).

the declarant is unlikely to misperceive or misremember their own state of mind or physical condition at the time but is more likely to misremember or fabricate later at trial. For similar reasons, a statement made for medical diagnosis or treatment that describes medical history, past or present symptoms, or potential causes is also an exception to the hearsay rule because a person seeking medical treatment is unlikely to be untruthful.[324]

4. Recorded Recollection

349. A recorded recollection about which the declarant once had knowledge is an exception to hearsay if the declarant now has insufficient recollection to enable full and accurate testimony about the matter.[325] The writing must have been made by the witness when the memory was still fresh, the witness must have firsthand knowledge of the incident, and the witness must testify that the record was accurate when made.

5. Business Records

350. Records made in the regular course of business are an exception to the hearsay rule.[326] In order to qualify under the exception, the record must have been made at or near the event and prepared in a trustworthy manner. The record must also have been one routinely made for the business and used in decision-making. The rationale for this exception is that the person making the record knows that the business relies on the accuracy of the record and that the record will be used by the business in its future operations and decisions.

6. Public Records

351. Similarly, an exception to the hearsay rule applies to records and reports of public offices or agencies setting forth activities of the office, matters observed pursuant to duty imposed by law, and statements and factual findings in civil actions and proceedings against the government.[327]

7. Other Exceptions

352. Other, less common exceptions to the hearsay rule are listed in the FRE.[328]

324. Fed. R. Evid. 803(4).
325. Fed. R. Evid. 803(5).
326. Fed. R. Evid. 803(6).
327. Fed. R. Evid. 803(8).
328. Fed. R. Evid. 803.

§6. WITNESS COMPETENCY

353. In order to give testimony, a witness must be considered competent. Competency is to be distinguished from credibility. Competency requires the witness to be able to possess the mental and physical capacity to perceive, record, recollect, and recount information, and is determined as a preliminary matter by the judge. Credibility goes to the weight the finder of fact assigns to the believability of the witness's testimony.[329]

354. Witnesses are competent to testify only to matters within their personal knowledge—things the witness actually observed, perceived, recorded, or recollects.[330] The purpose of the personal-knowledge rule is to reduce testimony containing speculations, rumors, opinions, and inferences, which may be better left for the finder of fact to draw at the conclusion of all testimony.

§7. OPINION TESTIMONY

I. Lay Opinion

355. At common law, non-expert witnesses were not permitted to give any opinion testimony. Instead, as suggested above, they were permitted to speak only on those facts of which they had personal knowledge. However, this proved to be an unrealistic constraint and many judges found it difficult to identify the line between fact and opinion. The rules today allow lay opinion testimony if the opinion is rationally based on the perception of the witness and the opinion is helpful to a clear understanding of the witness's testimony or the determination of a fact in issue.[331] To meet the first requirement, the party must first lay a foundation establishing personal knowledge of the facts which form the basis of the opinion or inference. Then, the party must also show that the opinion is rationally based on those facts and that any normal person would draw those same inferences from the same set of facts. The second requirement is easier to fulfill. If the judge finds that the testimony will aid the trier of fact even in a small way, the testimony should be admitted. Examples of admitted lay opinions include an opinion about a person's age based on objective appearances, about the speed of an automobile, or about a person's level of intoxication at a given time.

II. Expert Opinion Testimony

356. Experts may testify in the form of an opinion as well as give factual testimony, if the judge finds that the testimony will aid the jury in any way.[332] This

329. Fed. R. Evid. 601.
330. Fed. R. Evid. 602.
331. Fed. R. Evid. 701.
332. Fed. R. Evid. 702.

permits expert testimony where, even though the subject is well known to the average juror, the expert is able to draw a more reliable inference than a juror would without the aid of the expert's testimony.

357. Qualification as an expert is a matter for the judge to decide.[333] The expert must be sufficiently familiar with the theory or method underlying the opinion. The expert may not need not always possess academic degrees or specialized experience in a particular field.

358. One major point of contention between jurisdictions has been the level of reliability that scientific evidence must meet before it can be admitted by the trial judge. Before adoption of the FRE, the test announced in *Frye v. United States*[334] was the guiding principle used to answer that question. The *Frye* test required that the proffered evidence be based on a theory generally accepted among those in the field. This resulted in a substantial amount of relevant and reliable testimony being excluded because it was based on a theory not yet generally accepted. Although the federal courts no longer follow the *Frye* test, some states adhere to it.

359. Federal courts follow the test announced in *Daubert v.Merrell Dow Pharmaceuticals, Inc.*,[335] that expert evidence will be admitted if based upon sound methodology. Factors the trial court will consider include:

1. Whether the technique has survived peer review by publication in journals.
2. Whether there is any way to verify the results of the methodology.
3. The rate of error of the methodology.
4. Whether the methodology is generally accepted by the people in the scientific field to which it pertains.
5. Whether the opinion was developed expressly for the purpose of testifying or based on preexisting or independent research.

360. Experts may base their testimony on facts and data perceived by or made known to the expert at or before the hearing.[336] One common basis for expert opinions is the personal observations of the expert witness. However, experts may testify based on information reasonably relied upon by experts in the particular field in forming opinions or inferences about the subject, whether or not the outside information is itself admissible at trial. The facts and data relied upon may include documents, oral statements, treatises, and opinions or conclusions of others if that information is of the type the expert normally relies upon in reaching an opinion.

333. Fed. R. Evid. 104(a).
334. 293 F. 1013 (App. D.C. 1923).
335. 509 U.S. 579 (1993).
336. Fed. R. Evid. 703.

§8. IMPEACHMENT

361. Impeachment is evidence designed to impugn the credibility of other evidence. Both witnesses and documents can be impeached, but witnesses tend to be the primary subject of impeachment. Methods used to impeach a witness's credibility include attacking capacity, character, and bias of the witness; presenting evidence of a prior inconsistent statement; and pointing out a specific error in testimony. Impeachment may be during the cross-examination or through the introduction of other evidence or testimony.

Part V. Judgment Enforcement

Chapter 1. Preliminary Relief

§1. Introduction

362. Broadly speaking, courts are empowered to issue three types of injunctions: temporary restraining orders (TROs), preliminary injunctions, and permanent injunctions. The first two types are orders issued in the conduct of litigation, while the final type, the permanent injunction, is a form of judgment issued after full litigation of the merits of a civil action. This chapter deals with TROs and preliminary injunctions as part of the procedure for litigating a civil action in American courts. The law governing permanent injunctions is part of the substantive law of remedies, which is outside the scope of this work's discussion of American civil procedure. As with any other procedural matter, the procedures for granting or denying preliminary injunctions and TROs vary somewhat among the many American court systems. Most of the states, however, follow the guidelines for issuing TROs and preliminary injunctions set forth in the federal rules.

§2. Temporary Restraining Orders

363. A district court may issue a TRO without notice to the adverse party or ex parte. Because judicial action affecting one's legal rights without notice to that party is rare and may implicate constitutional due-process concerns, a TRO without notice has only a limited duration and is justified only for exigent circumstances.

364. The federal rules provide for a TRO when two prerequisites are met.[337] First, a TRO applicant must compellingly demonstrate via affidavit or verified complaint that irreparable damage, loss, or injury will occur before the opposing party or its attorney can be heard in opposition. An example of proper circumstances of irreparable harm is provided by a district court case, *Merrill Lynch v. Bishop*.[338] In that case, the plaintiff sufficiently supported its motion for a TRO when it showed that the defendant employee's use of the plaintiff's client lists was in violation of an employment agreement. However, another district court failed to find a sufficient showing of irreparable harm where a plaintiff, asserting an environmental interest,

337. Fed. R. Civ. P. 65(b).
338. *Merrill Lynch, Pierce, Fenner & Smith, Inc. v. Bishop*, 839 F. Supp. 68 (D. Me. 1993).

sought to enjoin the destruction of forty acres of timber because the plaintiff had visited the site once only and the tract was but a fraction of 260,000 acres of forest.[339] Second, a TRO applicant's attorney must certify to the court in writing what efforts the attorney has undertaken to notify adverse parties, accompanied by reasons why formal notice through service of process should not be required. In a 1968 case, the U.S. Supreme Court tacitly endorsed this practice, noting that its jurisprudence permits ex parte issuance of TROs but cautioning district courts that a TRO should not be issued without notice unless the movant's showing of irreparable harm is compelling and the movant has demonstrated that all reasonable efforts towards notice, including informal notice, have been exhausted.[340]

365. Once the movant has satisfied these prerequisites, the district court retains discretion whether or not to issue the TRO. If the court decides to grant the TRO, it must endorse the order with the date and time of issuance. So issued, the order lasts for no longer than ten days unless good cause can be shown for an extension. Next, the district court must schedule an adversarial hearing to consider a preliminary injunction "at the earliest possible time."[341] The hearing date takes precedence over all other court matters except for older matters of the same character. Finally, Rule 65(b) provides that after two day's notice, or such shorter time as the court prescribes, the adverse party may move and appear for the purpose of dissolving the order, modifying the order, or both. In such an event, Rule 65(b) requires the district court to conduct a hearing on the adverse party's motion "as expeditiously as the ends of justice require."[342]

§3. Preliminary Injunctions

366. A preliminary injunction is another form of intermediate relief.[343] It requires notice to the adverse party and may be of any duration not surpassing final judgment in the case, but otherwise, courts have generally applied the TRO standards in deciding whether to issue a preliminary injunction.

367. The U.S. Supreme Court has added a further limitation to a district court's power to issue injunctions. In *Grupo Mexicano de Desarollo, S.A. v. Alliance Bond Fund, Inc.*,[344] an investment group that had purchased unsecured notes issued by a Mexican toll-road operator alleged that the operator had defaulted on its obligations under the notes. The group sued for damages and sought a preliminary injunction to prevent the notes from being assigned to the Mexican government. The district court issued the requested injunction and the Second Circuit affirmed. The Supreme Court

339. *Donham v. U.S. Department of Agriculture*, 725 F. Supp. 985 (S.D. Ill. 1989).
340. *Carroll v. President & Commissioners of Princess Anne*, 393 U.S. 175 (1968); *Granny Goose Foods v. Brotherhood of Teamsters*, 415 U.S. 423 (1974); *Samson v. Murray*, 415 U.S. 61 (1974).
341. Fed. R. Civ. P. 65(b).
342. *Ibid.*
343. Fed. R. Civ. P. 65(a).
344. *Grupo Mexicano de Desarollo, S.A. v. Alliance Bond Fund, Inc.*, 527 U.S. 308 (1999).

reversed, holding that a district court lacked the power to issue a preliminary injunction regarding the disposition of assets incident to a mere damages action in which no lien or equitable claim had been asserted.

368. Once the court decides to issue a preliminary injunction or TRO, the applicant must post a bond in an amount the court deems proper to cover any possible damage the opponent may suffer as a result of a wrongful injunction.[345]

345. Fed. R. Civ. P. 65(c).

Chapter 2. Final Judgment

369. Enforcement of a final judgment occurs in different ways depending upon the type of judgment. Declaratory judgments and defense judgments are essentially self-enforcing because they need no subsequent enforcement procedures in order for the party obtaining the judgment to enjoy its benefits, though, if necessary, they can be enforced through doctrines of preclusion, discussed below. Other similar devices, such as quiet-title actions and some accountings, trigger automatic action by government officials, which is all the prevailing party needs to accomplish its objectives. And injunctions are enforceable ultimately through the court's power of contempt. If a party disobeys a direct judicial order, he can be tried, both civilly and criminally, for contempt.

370. Money judgments are often more difficult to enforce. They authorize the winning party to take coercive steps if payment on the judgment is not made by the losing party. Coercive steps include levying personal or real property, garnishing wages, or seizure of property. State law generally governs the use of these and other enforcement devices. In federal court, enforcement is governed by state law absent any governing federal law.

371. A judgment entered in one state is generally enforceable in another state because the U.S. Constitution's Full Faith and Credit Clause and its implementing statute obligate states to respect each other's valid judgments.[346] A winning party who wishes to enforce the judgment of one jurisdiction's court in another jurisdiction must first register the judgment with the court clerk in the enforcing jurisdiction. Once the judgment is registered, it will be enforced according to the rules and procedures of the enforcing jurisdiction. Local law will govern execution and other supplemental proceedings, such as time limitations on the life of the judgment and exemption of certain types of property from execution.

372. Another exception to the Full Faith and Credit Clause involves lack of jurisdiction. If the rendering court lacks either subject-matter or personal jurisdiction, its judgment is void and not entitled to enforcement in the alternate court. If, however, jurisdiction is litigated in the original litigation, and the original forum rules that it has jurisdiction, the enforcing forum may disallow relitigation of the jurisdictional claims. In other words, a party challenging jurisdiction ordinarily can challenge it in only one forum.

346. U.S. Const. Art. IV, §1; 28 U.S.C. §1738.

Part VI. Out-of-Court Dispute Resolution

Chapter 1. Arbitration

373. Arbitration is closest to civil litigation because it involves an adversarial presentation of cases before a neutral adjudicator. Arbitration is primarily a creature of contract—the parties consent to arbitration on specified terms. Although parties can, in theory, create their preferred arbitration system out of whole cloth, the rise of reputable arbitration services firms has led most parties to simply select a provider's rules and procedures.

374. Arbitration is seen as a lower-cost alternative to litigation because arbitration can be customized to the parties' and the case's needs with more streamlined discovery and tailored relief. Arbitration is also less formal than litigation—arbitration hearings typically take place in a conference room rather than a court. And arbitration is often nonpublic.

375. Because arbitration is a creature of contract, a party with disparate bargaining power can slant the arbitration procedures unfairly. For that reason, many states and courts historically exhibited hostility against arbitration agreements. But in 1925, Congress passed the Federal Arbitration Act (FAA), which codified a acceptance of arbitration as an effective and often cheaper alternative to civil litigation.[347] Under the FAA, arbitration agreements may not be singled out among contractual provisions for disfavored treatment, and, in a series of cases, the U.S. Supreme Court has aggressively enforced contractual freedom to arbitrate, striking down a variety of state laws purporting to hold arbitration agreements invalid.[348]

376. Today, arbitration is ubiquitous in all kinds of contracts, including consumer contracts of adhesion and contracts in click-consent electronic terms of service. Rarely, arbitration agreements are customized in ways that unfairly disadvantage a party with less bargaining power, but, more often, arbitration agreements select the procedures of reputable providers whose rules are generally neutral. A lingering concern is arbitration's focus on privatized justice, which discounts the public civil justice system's broader interests in deterrence. The funneling of public-interest cases to private, secret, streamlined arbitration may most adversely affect the public.

347. 9 U.S.C. §§1, et seq.
348. E.g., *AT&T Mobility LLC v. Concepcion*, 563 U.S. 333 (2011).

Chapter 2. Mediation

377. Mediation is a structured negotiation process facilitated by a third party. Acting as a "participant-observer," the mediator assesses the strengths and weaknesses of each side to encourage compromise and settlement between the parties. Mediation may be an especially useful method where the parties have an ongoing relationship or when more is at stake than money because a resolution could be tailored so that both sides come away winners.

378. Mediation procedure involves very informal case presentations to the mediator, usually without formal evidence. After the parties or their attorneys have presented a case statement, the parties caucus while the mediator shuttles between caucuses to find common ground and encourage compromise. The mediator is less interested in adjudication and truth-determination than in finding common ground for compatible resolution.

379. Mediation is regarded as very successful, especially in cases where the parties are participating voluntarily. Most mediation participants, 75% or more, are satisfied with the process even when an agreement is not reached. However, unlike arbitration, no federal law requires or regulates mediation.

Chapter 3. Negotiation

380. Negotiation is the most common dispute resolution method. It is informal and unregulated. The parties negotiate bilaterally, on their own terms and on their own timeframes, until they reach a mutually agreed resolution memorialized by a contract. Compromise is key. While direct negotiation ought to be the first option for resolving disputes, most parties file suit first and negotiate later. Sophisticated business parties, however, recognize that large gains may be achieved by seeking negotiated resolutions before resorting to litigation. Except in class actions, settlement terms are not reviewed by the judge and, in many cases, are kept confidential. Settlement thus successfully resolves private disputes but often at the expense of public interests in justice and deterrence.

Part VII. Ancillary Topics

Chapter 1. Applicable Law

381. In the American tradition, courts need not always apply the law of their own sovereign. When multiple sovereign interests are in play, the forum court must decide which sovereign's law to apply to resolve a dispute. The inquiry is styled as conflict of laws or, as it is also known, choice of law. Because this volume focuses on domestic civil procedure, it will not focus on questions of international conflict of laws or, as it is commonly called in other countries, private international law. Instead, this volume considers domestic choice of law, which, for a dual-sovereign federal system of a supreme national government and fifty quasi-sovereign governments, is complex enough. Although even domestic conflict of laws could generate its own volume and is usually taught as a separate course in American law schools, a brief summary here seems warranted because the topic intersects with other matters of procedure and jurisdiction.

382. A federal court hearing only federal law issues will apply only federal law to resolve them. However, because both diversity jurisdiction and supplemental jurisdiction allow federal courts to hear cases with state common-law claims, a conflict occasionally arises between how a state court would choose to resolve an issue and how a federal court would choose to resolve an issue. Say, for example, a case involving a claim of negligence was brought in federal court, and the case presented a novel question of whether a duty attached in a particular circumstance. Can the federal court decide on its own whether such a duty should attach? Or must the federal court do what it thinks a state court would decide? This situation presents a question of vertical choice of law.

383. Congress has, by statute, long directed federal courts to apply state law as rules of decision in cases where they apply and where federal law does not.[349] In the infamous case *Erie Railroad Co. v. Tompkins*,[350] the Supreme Court held that the statutory directive applied to state common law and that federal courts exercising diversity jurisdiction could not come up with their own rules of decision for general common-law questions. In the subsequent case, *Hanna v. Plumer*,[351] the Court held that codified federal law, including the Federal Rules of Civil Procedure, was

349. 28 U.S.C. §1652.
350. 304 U.S. 64 (1938).
351. 380 U.S. 460 (1965).

not subject to Congress's directive but instead applied in all cases unless otherwise invalid. Subsequent cases have developed some nuances to the doctrine—for example, the preclusive effect of a federal court judgment is determined by federal common law.[352] But as an oversimplified heuristic, vertical choice of law follows the rule that courts apply the substantive law of the claim and the procedural law of the forum.

384. The vertical determination that substantive state law applies to a claim does not resolve *which* state's law applies. That question involves choosing from among states with various interests in the dispute. Say, for example, a New Yorker was injured in a car accident in Massachusetts caused by a Connecticut driver. The New Yorker sues the Connecticut driver in Connecticut federal court. The federal court knows that it must apply state law to resolve the substantive tort claims and defenses. But should the federal court apply New York, Massachusetts, or Connecticut tort law? The answer is complicated and first depends upon what choice-of-law principles to apply. And in the absence of some federal law choosing from among states, the federal court must apply the same choice-of-law principles that a state court sitting in its state—here, New York—would apply. So, whatever law New York state courts would apply to the dispute must also be applied by the New York federal court.

385. What law state courts would apply is a question of horizontal choice of law, and different states have adopted different choice-of-law rules. For some issues, such as commercial contracts, states tend to adopt uniform rules, but for others, such as torts, states diverge widely on their choice-of-law methodology.

386. The rub is that the choice of court can also be a choice of law. Certainly, a party can choose federal procedural rules or state procedural rules by choosing between federal and state court. But a party also can often choose the substantive law by deciding in which state to sue. In an astonishing case called *Ferens v. John Deere Co.*,[353] a farmworker in Pennsylvania was injured when using a combine manufactured by John Deere, a Delaware corporation. The injury gave rise to both tort claims and breach of contract claims, and Pennsylvania was a good place for the farmworker to sue because it was convenient for him and because Pennsylvania law was, with one exception, also favorable to him. The one exception was that the Pennsylvania statute of limitations for tort claims was quite short, and by the time Ferens got around to filing his lawsuit, that deadline had passed. So, Ferens filed two lawsuits. He filed his contract claim in federal court in Pennsylvania, invoking the court's diversity jurisdiction. And he filed his tort claim in Mississippi federal court, also invoking diversity jurisdiction. (At the time, John Deere believed it was subject to general personal jurisdiction in Mississippi.) Why did Ferens choose Mississippi? Because the Mississippi federal court would apply Mississippi state choice of law rules to the claim, and Mississippi choice of law rules would use the law of the forum for purposes of the statute of limitations and the law of the state of injury

352. *Semtek International Inc. v. Lockheed Martin Corp.*, 531 U.S. 497 (2001).
353. 494 U.S. 516 (1990).

for the other issues in tort—i.e., the court would apply Mississippi's statute of limitations and Pennsylvania tort law. And Ferens had discovered that Mississippi's statute of limitations was still running. Ferens now had two separate cases, but he then cleverly asked the Mississippi federal court to transfer the case—for the convenience of the parties and witnesses—to Pennsylvania, where he was located, where the accident happened, and where, after all, a related case was pending! The Mississippi court did so, and his two cases were consolidated before the same judge. So Ferens got his preferred forum, his preferred Pennsylvania law, and his preferred statute of limitations. The Supreme Court upheld his gamesmanship.

Chapter 2. Recusal

387. Traditionally, two terms have been used to describe removal of a judge from hearing a case: recusal and disqualification. "Recusal" refers to situations where a judge decides to stand down voluntarily. "Disqualification," by contrast, describes occasions when a party to the litigation challenges, by statutorily or constitutionally authorized motion, a judge's participation. While historically distinct, the terms are used interchangeably by modern jurisdictions and governing statutes.

388. Generally, American law provides two grounds for disqualification of a judge for cause: constitutional due-process concerns and statutory provisions. Due-process concerns stem from a fundamental guarantee to all litigants of a fair and impartial trial.[354] Therefore, in cases where a judge's self-interest may prejudice his or her conduct during the course of trial, litigants may challenge that judge's continuing role in the proceedings.

389. In federal court, a judge must recuse from any proceeding where judicial impartiality might reasonably be questioned.[355] Recusal is required where a judge has a personal prejudice or bias towards a party; has personal knowledge of the proceeding's evidentiary facts; has served as a lawyer in private practice in the matter before him; has worked with a lawyer currently associated with the proceeding; where either the judge or a lawyer he worked with is a material witness in the proceeding; where the judge, working as a government employee, participated as counsel, adviser, or witness in the proceeding; or where the judge has a financial or other interest that could be substantially affected by the outcome of the proceeding. Recusal should be considered when the judge, the judge's spouse, or a relation of either is a party, lawyer, or witness in the proceeding.

390. A particularly detailed and thought-provoking, if controversial, illustration can be found in *Cheney v. United States District Court*,[356] where Justice Scalia attempted to justify his decision to hear a case involving Vice President Richard Cheney notwithstanding the personal relationship between the Vice President and Justice Scalia.

354. *See, e.g.*, *Tumey v. Ohio*, 273 U.S. 510, 523 (1927).
355. 28 U.S.C. §455.
356. *Cheney v. United States District Court*, 541 U.S. 913 (2004) (in chambers opinion of Scalia, J.).

Chapter 3. Rulemaking

391. The Federal Rules of Civil Procedure apply to civil cases in federal district court, and so a few words about how they are drafted seems a fitting conclusion to this volume.

392. Promulgating prospective rules of court is functionally a legislative power, not a judicial power. Further, Congress's power to "ordain and establish" the lower federal courts implies the power to create rules of court procedure for them.[357] Finally, Congress's power under the Necessary and Proper Clause arguably provides authority to implement the judicial power wielded by lower federal courts.[358] Perhaps some limits on Congress's authority to provide for court procedure exist, but, in the main, court rulemaking power is Congress's.

393. Congress, however, does not always understand the business of civil litigation as well as the courts. Accordingly, Congress has delegated rulemaking power to the Supreme Court. In the Rules Enabling Act, Congress has given the Supreme Court the "power to prescribe general rules of practice and procedure and rules of evidence" for the lower courts, as long as the rules do not "abridge, enlarge or modify any substantive right."[359]

394. To provide for transparency and a residual measure of congressional control, Congress has provided a reticulated process for rulemaking. The Judicial Conference, an administrative body for the courts comprised of sitting federal judges, has appointed a Standing Committee on rules of practice and procedure and an Advisory Committee on civil rules, each of whose members are appointed by the Chief Justice.

395. Anyone can submit a proposed rule or rule amendment to the Standing Committee. Each suggestion, along with the submitter's name and address, is publicly available. The Standing Committee refers suggestions pertaining to the Federal Rules of Civil Procedure to the Advisory Committee.

396. The Advisory Committee will then consider the suggestions, along with its own suggestions. All committee meetings are, by default, with advance notice and open to the public, and all committee discussions of a proposal are recorded in detailed meeting minutes and agenda books, which are publicly available.

397. If the Advisory Committee decides to move forward with a proposal, it will publish a draft amendment, explanatory note, and basis for recommendation, including evaluation of any competing considerations. The Advisory Committee submits the proposal to the Standing Committee for its approval and publishes the materials on the U.S. Courts website.

357. U.S. Const. Art. III, §1.
358. U.S. Const. Art. I, §8, cl. 16.
359. 28 U.S.C. §2072.

398. Upon Standing Committee approval, the Standing Committee will circulate the proposal as widely as possible to the bench, bar, and public. The Standing Committee will also notify members of Congress, federal judges, and state judges. A public-comment period then begins.

399. The public-comment period must extend for at least six months, during which the Advisory Committee holds public hearings on the amendment and interested parties submit comments supporting or opposing the amendment. All hearings are recorded and all comments are posted on the U.S. Courts website. When the comment period closes, the committee creates a report of the written comments and hearing testimony.

400. The Advisory Committee then considers any revisions in light of the comments. Substantial revisions usually undergo a second notice-and-comment period. Upon conclusion of any revisions, the committee then submits a report and recommendation to the Standing Committee, which will consider the amendment at a public meeting. If the Standing Committee approves, it will forward the amendment proposal to the Judicial Conference, and if the Judicial Conference approves, it will forward the proposal to the U.S. Supreme Court.

401. The Supreme Court rarely rejects amendment proposals. Upon approval, the Court transmits them to Congress by May 1 of a given year. Congress then has until December 1 to act to delay or override the amendments. Absent congressional action, the amendments become law on December 1.

402. The transparent and participatory process is designed to ensure rules that reflect the ideals in Rule 1 of the Federal Rules of Civil Procedure: "the just, speedy, and inexpensive determination of every action and proceeding."[360] Whether American civil litigation has achieved those goals is beyond the scope of this volume.

360. Fed. R. Civ. P. 1.

Selected Bibliography

Books

Baude, William et al., *Hart and Wechsler's The Federal Courts and the Federal System*. 8th edn. New York: Foundation Press, 2025.

Bodenheimer, Edgar, John Bilyeu Oakley & Jean C. Love, *An Introduction to the Anglo-American Legal System*. 4th edn. St. Paul: West Publishing, 2004.

Burch, Elizabeth Chamblee, *Mass Tort Deals: Backroom Bargaining in Multidistrict Litigation*. Cambridge: Cambridge University Press, 2019.

Chase, Oscar, et al., *Civil Litigation in Comparative Context*. 2nd edn. New York: West Academic, 2017.

Damaška, Mirjan R., *The Faces of Justice and State Authority: A Comparative Approach to the Legal Process*. New Haven: Yale University Press, 1986.

Flamm, Richard E., *Judicial Disqualification: Recusal and Disqualification of Judges* (2017). 3rd edn. Berkeley, CA: Banks & Jordan Law Publishing.

Friedman, Lawrence M., *A History of American Law*. 3rd edn. New York: Simon & Schuster, 2005.

Hazard, Jr, Geoffrey C. & Michele Taruffo, *American Civil Procedure: An Introduction*. New Haven: Yale University Press, 1993.

Hazard, Jr, Geoffrey C. et al., *Cases and Materials on Pleading and Procedure: State and Federal*. 9th edn. New York: Foundation Press, 2005.

Holmes, Jr, Oliver Wendell, *The Common Law*. Rev. edn. Mineola: Dover Publications, 1991.

Kagan, Robert A., *Adversarial Legalism: The American Way of Law*. 2nd edn. Cambridge: Harvard University Press, 2019.

Lacey, Frederick B. & Jay G. Safer, "The Authority, Roles, Responsibilities and Utilization of Magistrate Judges." In *Business and Commercial Litigation in Federal Courts*, vol. 2. Edited by Robert L. Haig. Chicago: American Bar Association, 1998.

Lookofsky, Joseph M., *Transnational Litigation and Commercial Arbitration: A Comparative Analysis of American, European, and International law*. 2nd edn. Huntington: Juris Publications, 2004.

Madison, James, Alexander Hamilton & John Jay, *The Federalist Papers*. Edited by Clinton Rossiter. New York: Signet Classics, 2003.

Meador, Daniel John, *American Courts*. 2nd edn. St. Paul: West Publishing Co., 2001.

Meador, Daniel John, *Appellate Courts in the United States*. 2nd edn. St. Paul: West Publishing Co., 2006.
Moore, James W. et al., *Moore's Federal Practice*. 3rd edn. New York: Mathew Bender, 1997-2000 (date varies by volume).
Saari, David J., *American Court Management: Theories and Practices*. Westport, CO: Quorum Books, 1982.
Smith, Christopher E. *Judicial Self Interest: Federal Judges and Court Administration*. New York: Praeger, 1995.
Wood, Gordon S., *The Creation of the American Republic, 1776–1789*. Chapel Hill: University of North Carolina Press, 1969.
Wright, Charles Alan et al., *Federal Practice and Procedure*. 4th edn. St. Paul: West Publishing Co., 2006–2020 (date and edition varies by volume).

Articles

Arnold, Tom, "A Vocabulary of ADR Procedures," ALI-ABA C976 (1994): 19.
Arthur, Thomas C. & Richard D. Freer, "Grasping at Burnt Straws: The Disaster of the Supplemental Jurisdiction Statute," Emory L. J. 40 (1991): 963.
Bermant, Gordon & Russell R. Wheeler, "Federal Judges and the Judicial Branch: Their Independence and Accountability," Mercer L. Rev. 46 (1995): 835.
Bone, Robert G., "The Process of Making Process: Court Rulemaking, Democratic Legitimacy, and Procedural Efficacy," Geo. L. J. 87 (1999): 887.
Bradt, Andrew D. & D. Theodore Rave, "Aggregation on Defendants' Terms: *Bristol-Myers Squibb* and the Federalization of Mass-Tort Litigation," B.C. L. Rev. 59 (2018): 1251.
Bradt, Andrew D. & D. Theodore Rave, "It's Good to Have the 'Haves' On Your Side: A Defense of Repeat Players in Multidistrict Litigation," Geo. L. J. 108 (2019): 73.
Bradt, Andrew D. & Lynn A. Baker, "MDL Myths," Tex. L. Rev. 101 (2023): 1521.
Bradt, Andrew D., "'A Radical Proposal': The Multidistrict Litigation Act of 1968," U. Pa. L. Rev. 165 (2017): 831.
Bradt, Andrew D., "The Long Arm of Multidistrict Litigation," Wm. & Mary L. Rev. 59 (2018): 1166.
Brunet, Edward, "The Timing of Summary Judgment," F.R.D. 198 (2001): 679.
Burbank, Stephen B., "Interjurisdictional Preclusion and Federal Common Law: Toward a General Approach," Cornell L. Rev. 70 (1985): 625.
Burbank, Stephen B., "Pleading and the Dilemmas of 'General Rules,'" Wis. L. Rev. 2009 (2009): 535.
Burbank, Stephen B., "Proportionality and the Benefits of Discovery: Out of Sight, Out of Mind?," Rev. Litig. 35 (2016): 647.
Burbank, Stephen B., "Proposals to Amend Rule 68—Time to Abandon Ship," U. Mich. J .L. Reform 19 (1986): 425.
Burbank, Stephen B., "*Semtek*, Forum Shopping and Federal Common Law," Notre Dame L. Rev. 77 (2002): 1027.
Burbank, Stephen B., "The Class Action Fairness Act of 2005 in Historical Context: A Preliminary View," U. Pa. L. Rev. 156 (2008): 1439.
Burbank, Stephen B., "The Rules Enabling Act of 1934," U. Pa. L. Rev. 130 (1982): 1015.

Burbank, Stephen B., "The Transformation of American Civil Procedure: The Example of Rule 11," U. Pa. L. Rev. 137 (1989): 1925.
Burbank, Stephen B., "The World in Our Courts," Mich. L. Rev. 89 (1991): 1456.
Burbank, Stephen B., "Vanishing Trials and Summary Judgment in Federal Civil Cases: Drifint Towards Bethlehem or Gomorrah?" J. Emp. Legal Stud. 1 (2004): 591.
Burbank, Stephen, "Procedure, Politics and Power: The Role of Congress," Notre Dame L. Rev. 79 (2004): 1677.
Burch, Elizabeth Chamblee & Margaret S. Williams, "Repeat Players in Multidistrict Litigation: The Social Network," Cornell L. Rev. 102 (2017): 1445.
Burch, Elizabeth Chamblee, "Constructing Issue Classes," Va. L. Rev. 101 (2015): 1855.
Campbell, Jr, Robert S. et al., ABA Committee on Federal Civil Procedure, "The Importance of the Twelve-Member Jury in Federal Courts," F.R.D. 205 (2003): 247.
Carrington, Paul D., "Continuing Work on the Civil Rules: The Summons," Notre Dame L. Rev. 63 (2014): 733.
Chayes, Abram, "The Role of the Judge in Public Law Litigation," Harv. L. Rev. 89 (1976): 1281.
Clopton, Zachary D. & D. Theodore Rave, "MDL in the States," Nw. U. L. Rev. 115 (2021): 1649.
Clopton, Zachary D., "Long Arm 'Statutes,'" Green Bag 2d 23 (2020): 89.
Coffee, Jr, John C., "Class Wars: The Dilemma of the Mass Tort Class Action," Colum. L. Rev. 95 (1995): 1343.
Dalton, Harlon Leigh, "Taking the Right to Appeal (More or Less) Seriously," Yale L. J. 95 (1985): 62.
Deja, Daniel R., "How Judges are Selected: A Survey of the Judicial Selection Process in the United States," Mich. B. J. 75 (1996): 904.
Dodge, William S. & Scott Dodson, "Personal Jurisdiction and Aliens," Mich. L. Rev. 116 (2018): 1205.
Dodge, William S., Christopher A. Whytock & Maggie Gardner, "The Many State Doctrines of Forum Non Conveniens," Duke L. J. 72 (2023): 1163.
Dodson, Scott & Phillip A. Pucillo, "Joint and Several Jurisdiction," Duke L. J. 65 (2016): 1323.
Dodson, Scott & Sebastian Spinei, "Judicial Jurisdiction and Competence." In *Handbook on Comparative Civil Procedure*. Edited by Remco van Rhee & Margaret Woo. London: Edward Elgar, 2025.
Dodson, Scott, "Accountability and Transparency in U.S. Courts." In *Accountability and Transparency in Civil Justice*. Edited by Daniel Mitidiero. New York: Thomson Reuters, 2019.
Dodson, Scott, "*Atlantic Marine* and the Future of Party Preference," Hastings L. J. 66 (2015): 675.
Dodson, Scott, "Beyond Bias in Diversity Jurisdiction Jurisdiction," Duke L. J. 69 (2019): 267.
Dodson, Scott, "Cooperativism in the American Adversarial Tradition," Civ. Just. Q. 40 (2021): 283.
Dodson, Scott, "In Search of Removal Jurisdiction," Nw. U. L. Rev. 102 (2008): 55.

Dodson, Scott, "Jurisdiction and Its Effects," Geo. L. J. 105 (2017): 619.
Dodson, Scott, "Personal Jurisdiction and Aggregation," Nw. U. L. Rev. 113 (2018): 1.
Dodson, Scott, "Personal Jurisdiction in Comparative Context," Am. J. Comp. L. 68 (2020): 701.
Dodson, Scott, "Rule 4 and Personal Jurisdiction," Notre Dame L. Rev. 99 (2024): 1.
Dodson, Scott, "The Complexities of Consent to Personal Jurisdiction," Calif. L. Rev. 113 (2025): 333.
Dodson, Scott, "The Gravitational Force of Federal Law," U. Pa. L. Rev. 164 (2016): 703.
Dodson, Scott, "The Supreme Court and Public Opinion," Iowa. L. Rev. 111 (2025).
Dodson, Scott, "Why Do In-State Plaintiffs Invoke Diversity Jurisdiction?," L. & Soc. Inquiry 49 (2024): 1283.
Dubois, Philip L., "Accountability, Independence, and the Selection of State Judges: The Role of Popular Judicial Elections," Sw. L. J. 40 (1986): 31.
Edwards, Harry T., "Alternative Dispute Resolution: Panacea or Anathema," Harv. L. Rev. 99 (1986): 668.
Eisenberg, Theodore, et al., "Juries, Judges and Punitive Damages," Cornell L. Rev. 87 (2002): 743.
Fairman, Christopher M., "The Myth of Notice Pleading," Ariz. L. Rev. 45 (2003): 987.
Fiss, Owen M., "Against Settlement," Yale L.J. 93 (1984): 1073.
Floyd, C. Douglas, "The Limits of Minimal Diversity," Hastings L. J. 55 (2004): 613.
Freer, Richard D., "Of Rules and Standards: Reconciling the Statutory Limitations on 'Arising Under' Jurisdiction," Ind. L. J. 82 (2007): 309.
Freer, Richard D., "Rethinking Compulsory Joinder: A Proposal to Restructure Federal Rule 19," N.Y.U. L. Rev. 60 (1985): 1061.
Freer, Richard D., "The Cauldron Boils: Supplemental Jurisdiction, Amount in Controversy, and Diversity of Citizenship Class Actions," Emory L. J. 53 (2004): 55.
Freer, Richard D., "The State of *Erie* After *Gasperini*," Tex. L. Rev. 76 (1998): 1637.
Freer, Richard D., "Toward a Principled Statutory Approach to Supplemental Jurisdiction in Diversity of Citizenship Cases," Ind. L. J. 74 (1998): 5.
Friedenthal, Jack & Joshua Gardner, "Judicial Discretion to Deny Summary Judgment in the Era of Managerial Judging," Hofstra L. Rev. 31 (2002): 91.
Frost, Amanda, "The Limits of Advocacy," Duke L. J. 59 (2009): 447.
Galanter, Mark, "The Vanishing Trial: An Examination of Trials and Related Matters in State and Federal Courts," J. Emp. Legal Stud. 1 (2004): 459.
Gardner, Maggie, "Retiring Forum Non Conveniens," N.Y.U. L. Rev. 92 (2017): 390.
Gluck, Abbe R. & Elizabeth Chamblee Burch, "MDL Revolution," N.Y.U. L. Rev. 96 (2021): 1.
Grodin, Joseph R., "Developing a Consensus of Constraint: A Judge's Perspective on Judicial Retention Elections," S. Cal. L. Rev. 61 (1988): 1969.
Grossi, Simona, "The Claim," Hous. L. Rev. 55 (2017): 1.

Hadfield, Jilian, "Where Have All the Trials Gone?," J. Empir. Legal Stud. 1 (2004): 705.

Hartnett, Edward A., "Taming *Twombly*, Even After *Iqbal*," U. Pa. L. Rev. 158 (2010): 473.

Issacharoff, Samuel, "Rule 23 and the Triumph of Experience," L. & Contemp. Probs. 84 (2021): 161.

Issacharoff, Samuel, "The Governance Problem in Aggregate Litigation," Fordham L. Rev. 81 (2013): 3165.

Kahan, Dan M., David A. Hoffman & Donald Braman, "Whose Eyes are you Going to Believe? Scott v. Harris and the Perils of Cognitive Illiberalism," Harv. L. Rev. 122 (2009): 837.

Keeling, Byron C., "Toward a Balanced Approach to 'Frivolous' Litigation: A Critical Review of Federal Rule 11 and State Sanctions Provisions," Pepperdine L. Rev. 21 (1994): 1067.

Kirgis, Paul F., "The Right to a Jury Decision on Questions of Fact under the Seventh Amendment," Ohio St. L. J. 64 (2003): 1125.

La Belle, Megan M., "Personal Jurisdiction and the Fairness Factor(s)," Emory L. J. 72 (2023): 781.

Leute, Sheila A., "The Effective Use of Summary Judgment: A Comparison of Federal and Texas Standards," Baylor L. Rev. 40 (1988): 617.

Lilly, Graham, "The Decline of the American Jury," U. Colo. L. Rev. 72 (2001): 53.

Lookofsky, Joseph M., Transnational Litigation and Commercial Arbitration: A Comparative Analysis of American, European, and International Law. 2nd edn. Huntington, New York: Juris Publications, 2004.

Macey, Jonathan R. & Geoffrey P. Miller, "The Plaintiffs' Attorney's Role in Class Action and Derivative Litigation: Economic Analysis and Recommendations for Reform," U. Chi. L. Rev. 58 (1991): 1.

Marcus, David, "The History of the Modern Class Action, Part I: Sturm und Drang, 1953–1980," Wash. U. L. Rev. 90 (2013): 587.

Marcus, David, "The Short Life and Long Afterlife of the Mass Tort Class Action," U. Pa. L. Rev. 165 (2017): 1565.

Marcus, David, "The History of the Modern Class Action, Part II: Litigation and Legitimacy, 1981–1994," Fordham L. Rev. 86 (2018): 1785.

Marcus, David, "Trans-Substantivity and the Process of American Law," B.Y.U. L. Rev. 2013 (2013): 1191.

Marcus, Richard, "Cure-All for an Era of Dispersed Litigation? Toward a Maximalist Use of the Multidistrict Litigation Panel's Transfer Power," Tulane L. Rev. 62 (2008): 2245.

Marcus, Richard, "Discovery Containment Redux," B. C. L. Rev. 39 (1998): 747

Marcus, Richard, "Only Yesterday: Reflections on Rulemaking Responses to E-Discovery," Fordham L. Rev. 73 (2004): 1.

Marcus, Richard, "Putting American Procedural Exceptionalism into a Globalized Context," Am. J. Comp. L. 53 (2005): 709.

Marcus, Richard, "Reassessing the Essential Role of Public Courts: Learning from the American Experience." In *Transformation of Civil Justice: Unity and Diversity*. Edited by Alan Ezelac & Remco van Rhee. Princeton: Springer, 2018.

Marcus, Richard, "The Electronic Lawyer," DePaul L. Rev. 58 (2009): 263.

Marcus, Richard, "The Perils of Privilege: Waiver and the Litigator," Mich. L. Rev. 84 (1986): 1605.

Marcus, Richard, "The Puzzling Persistence of Pleading Practice," Tex. L. Rev. 76 (1998): 1749.

Marcus, Richard, "The Revival of Fact Pleading Under the Federal Rules of Civil Procedure," Colum. L. Rev. 86 (1986): 433.

Martland, David A., "Justice without Favor: Due Process and Separation of Executive and Judicial Powers in State Government," Yale L. J. 94 (1985): 1675.

McFarland, Douglas D., "Dictum Run Wild: How Long-Arm Statutes Extended to the Limits of Due Process," B.U. L. Rev. 84 (2004): 491.

McGovern, Frances E., "An Analysis of Mass Torts for Judges," Tex. L. Rev. 73 (1995): 1821.

Menkel-Meadow, Carrie, "When Dispute Resolution Begets Disputes of Its Own: Conflicts Among Dispute Professionals," UCLA L. Rev. 44 (1997): 1871.

Meyer, Judith P., "The Pros and Cons of Mediation," Disp. Resol. J. 52-Sum (1997): 8.

Miller, Arthur R., "Confidentiality, Protective Orders, and Public Access to the Courts," Harv. L. Rev. 105 (1991): 428.

Miller, Arthur R., "From *Conley* to *Twombly* to *Iqbal*: A Double Play on the Federal Rules of Civil Procedure," Duke L.J. 60 (2010): 1.

Miller, Arthur R., "Of Frankenstein Monsters and Shining Knights: Myth, Reality and the 'Class Action Problem,'" Harv. L. Rev. 92 (1979): 664.

Miller, Arthur R., "Simplified Pleading, Meaningful Days in Court, and Trials on the Merits: Reflections on the Deformation of Federal Procedure," N.Y.U. L. Rev. 88 (2013): 286.

Miller, Arthur R., "The New Certification Standard Under Rule 11," F.R.D. 130 (1990): 479.

Miller, Arthur R., "The Preservation and Rejuvenation of Aggregate Litigation: A Systemic Imperative," Emory L. J. 64 (2014): 293.

Moller, Mark & Lawrence B. Solum, "The Article III 'Party' and the Originalist Case Against Corporate Diversity Jurisdiction," Wm. & Mary L. Rev. 64 (2023): 1345.

Mullenix, Linda S., "The Counter-Reformation in Procedural Justice," Minn. L. Rev. 77 (1992): 375.

Nagareda, Richard A., "Class Certification in the Age of Aggregate Proof," N.Y.U. L. Rev. 84 (2009): 97.

Nagareda, Richard A., "Embedded Aggregation in Civil Litigation," Cornell L. Rev. 95 (2010): 1105.

Oakley, John B., "Federal Jurisdiction and the Problem of the Litigative Unit: When Does What 'Arise Under' Federal Law?," Tex. L. Rev. 76 (1998): 1829.

Oakley, John B., "Integrating Supplemental Jurisdiction and Diversity Jurisdiction: A Progress Report on the Work of the American Law Institute," Ind. L. J. 74 (1998): 25.

Pfander, James E., "Protective Jurisdiction, Aggregate Litigation, and the Limits of Article III," Calif. L. Rev. 95 (2007): 1423.

Prakash, Saikrishna & Stephen D. Smith, "How to Remove a Federal Judge," Yale L. J. 116 (2006): 72.

Purdue, Wendy Collins, "The Supplemental Jurisdiction Statute: Flawed but Flexible," Emory L. J. 41 (1992): 69.

Redish, Martin H., "Reassessing the Allocation of Judicial Business Between State and Federal Courts: Federal Jurisdiction and 'The Martian Chronicles,'" Va. L. Rev. 78 (1992): 1769.

Rehnquist, William H., "L. Ralph Meacham & Federal Courts Administration: A Decade of Innovation and Progress," Am. U. L. Rev. 44 (1995): 1477.

Resnik, Judith, "Managerial Judges," Harv. L. Rev. 96 (1982): 374.

Reynolds, William L., "The Iron Law of Full Faith and Credit," Md. L. Rev. 53 (1994): 412.

Rowe, Jr., Thomas D., Stephen B. Burbank & Thomas M. Mengler, "Compounding or Creating Confusion About Supplemental Jurisdiction? A Reply to Professor Freer," Emory L. J. 40 (1991): 943.

Sabatino, Jack M., "ADR as 'Litigation Lite': Procedural and Evidentiary Norms Embedded Within Alternative Dispute Resolution," Emory L. J. 47 (1998): 1289.

Sachs, Stephen E., "*Pennoyer* was Right," Tex. L. Rev. 125 (2017): 1249.

Sachs, Stephen E., "The Unlimited Jurisdiction of the Federal Courts," Va. L. Rev. 106 (2020): 1703.

Sander, Frank, "Varieties of Dispute Precessing," F.R.D. 70 (1976): 111.

Seinfeld, Gil, "The Federal Courts as a Franchise: Rethinking the Justifications for Federal-Question Jurisdiction," Calif. L. Rev. 97 (2009): 1.

Shapiro, David L., "An Incomplete Discussion of 'Arising Under' Jurisdiction," Notre Dame L. Rev. 91 (2016): 1931.

Shapiro, David L., "Federal Diversity Jurisdiction: A Survey and a Proposal," Harv. L. Rev. 91 (1977): 317.

Shepherd, Joanna M., "The Influence of Retention Politics on Judges' Voting," J. Legal Stud. 169 (2009): 38.

Spencer, A. Benjamin, "Plausibility Pleading," B. C. L. Rev. 49 (2008): 431.

Spencer, A. Benjamin, "Pleading Conditions of the Mind Under Rule 9(b)," Cardozo L. Rev. 41 (2020): 1015.

Spencer, A. Benjamin, "Rationalizing Cost Allocation in Civil Discovery," Rev. Litig. 34 (2015): 769.

Spencer, A. Benjamin, "The Territorial Reach of the Federal Courts," Fla. L. Rev. 71 (2019): 979.

Steinman, Adam N., "Access to Justice, Rationality, and Personal Jurisdiction," Vand. L. Rev. 71 (2018): 1401.

Steinman, Adam N., "The Irrepressible Myth of *Celotex*: Reconsidering Summary Judgment Burdens Twenty Years after the Trilogy," Wash. & Lee L. Rev. 63 (2006): 81.

Steinman, Adam N., "The Pleading Problem," Stan. L. Rev. 62 (2010): 1293.

Steinman, Adam N., "The Rise and Fall of Plausibility Pleading?," Vand. L. Rev. 69 (2016): 333.

Steinman, Adam N., "What Is the *Erie* Doctrine? (And What Does It Mean for the Contemporary Politics of Judicial Federalism?)," Notre Dame L. Rev. 84 (2008): 245.

Stempel, Jeffrey, "A Distorted Mirror: The Supreme Court's Shimmering View of Summary Judgment, Directed Verdict, and the Adjudication Process," Ohio St. L. J. 49 (1988): 96.
Thomas, Suja A., "The Fallacy of Dispositive Procedure," B. C. L. Rev. 50 (2009): 759.
Thomas, Suja A., "The Seventh Amendment, Modern Procedure and the English Common Law," Wash. U. L. Q. 82 (2004): 687.
Thomas, Suja A., "Why Summary Judgment is Unconstitutional," Va. L. Rev. 93 (2007): 139.
Thomas, Suja A., "Why the Motion to Dismiss is Now Unconstitutional," Minn. L. Rev. 92 (2008): 1851.
Tidmarsh, Jay, "The English Fire Courts and the American Right to Civil Jury Trial," U. Chi. L. Rev. 83 (2016): 1893.
Tobias, Carl, "The Past and Future of the Federal Rules in State Courts," Nev. L. J. 3 (2002): 400.
Twitchell, Mary, "The Myth of General Jurisdiction," Harv. L. Rev. 101 (1988): 610.
Wolfram, Charles W., "The Constitutional History of the Seventh Amendment," Minn. L. Rev. 57 (1973): 639.
Woolley, Patrick, "The Sources of Federal Preclusion Law after *Semtek*," U. Cin. L. Rev. 72 (2003): 527.
Yamamoto, Eric, Katherine G. Leonard & Shawna Sodersten, "Summary Judgment at the Crossroads: The Impact of the *Celotex* Trilogy," U. Haw. L. Rev. 12 (1990): 1.
Zambrano, Diego A., "Discovery as Regulation," Mich. L. Rev. 120 (2020): 71.

Websites/Reports

American Law Institute, www.ali.org/.
National Center for State Courts, www.ncsconline.org/.
US Courts, www.uscourts.gov.

Index

The numbers here refer to paragraph numbers.

Index

www.ingramcontent.com/pod-product-compliance
Lightning Source LLC
Chambersburg PA
CBHW071349230926
51846CB00002B/486
9789403546193